Real Estate Sales Meetings

Llani O'Connor   *Director of Publishing*

Peg Keilholz   *Book Editor*

Meg Givhan   *Production*

Real Estate Sales Meetings

Techniques and Topics

REALTORS®NATIONAL MARKETING INSTITUTE
of the
NATIONAL ASSOCIATION OF REALTORS®
Chicago, Illinois

International Standard Book Number: 0-913652-08-3
Library of Congress Catalog Card Number: 76-42903
Marketing Institute Catalog Number: BK 118

Printed in the United States of America
First printing, 1976, 5,000
  10 9 8 7 6 5 4 3 2 1

Data "Hierarchy of Needs" from MOTIVATION AND
PERSONALITY, 2nd edition by Abraham H. Maslow
Copyright © 1970 by Abraham H. Maslow
By permission of Harper & Row, Publishers, Inc.

Appendix 3 in THE PRACTICE OF CREATIVITY,
by George M. Prince
Copyright © 1970 by George M. Prince
By permission of Harper & Row, Publishers, Inc.

Foreword

This is not a book about how sales meetings work. What ought to happen in sales meetings and what does happen are two different things, often worlds apart. What this book can help you do is to make *your* sales meetings more effective than they are now.

To do this you need to

Have an objective for each meeting
Spend time on preparation
Conduct it well and
Follow up.

If you want your salespeople to work for you and for themselves more effectively, study this book and adapt it to your needs. Don't *talk* about what you're going to do. Do it. And don't pass this book around to your staff. It's *your* reference book. They'll wonder what you've read or how you came to make the sales meetings so much better. Keep them guessing about that. But keep them informed about the things that really matter.

Getting more listings
Making more sales
Having more satisfied buyers and sellers
Getting more referrals.

That's what adds up to more dollars in your pocket and theirs.

Acknowledgment

This book was planned and produced as a project of the Book Subcommittee of the REALTORS® NATIONAL MARKETING INSTITUTE Publications Committee.

Peg Keilholz, Book Editor for the Marketing Institute, researched and wrote the book.

A project consulting group worked closely with the editor from the book's inception to its completion. Members were chosen for their knowledge of the subject and their relevant practical experience. They gave liberally of their time and experience to develop a detailed outline, acted as resource people and identified others who were qualified to contribute valuable insights and experience. The manuscript was reviewed for both accuracy and credibility by the chairpersons and the project consulting group listed below.

Albert J. Mayer III, C.R.B.,
  R.M.
Cincinnati, OH
Chairperson, Publications
  Committee

David B. Doeleman, C.R.B.
Portland, OR
Chairperson, Book
  Subcommittee

Lydia Franz, G.R.I., C.R.B.
Barrington, IL
Chairperson, Project
  Consulting Group

Marion Blackwell, Jr., C.C.I.M.
Atlanta, GA

Gary Fugere, G.R.I.
Minneapolis, MI

Gordon Greene
Chicago, IL

Talova L. Jones, G.R.I.
Edmond, OK

Wallace Malmborg, G.R.I.
Geneva, IL

Contents

Introduction

"I know my meetings aren't what they should be," you say, "and I don't know where to begin to make them better." You're in good company. We interviewed REALTORS® all over the United States to gather material for this book. They mentioned over and over again having feelings of guilt because their sales meetings aren't better. Even the best want to improve.

No one can have consistently good sales meetings. You're doing well if you have really fine meetings about 60 percent of the time. But whether this week's meeting is good or not so good, you should never quit trying to make them better. This book will help you do a better job of planning and conducting sales meetings.

Sales meetings don't require some special, mystical knowledge. Like everything else in business, when they are handled well they involve a sure sense of what it is you want to achieve, careful planning and preparation and a certain amount of know-how in communications and conducting meetings. The basics are all here, ready to adapt to your needs and to use in your own way.

This reference book for brokers and sales managers brings together for the first time a variety of experiences and ideas from REALTORS® plus suggestions and inspiration from people in other fields. There is a wealth of suggested reading in books and periodicals and study courses in the real estate profession.

If you have time, read through the book now. If you're pressed for time, look at the table of contents and the index to find where to turn for specific kinds of help on whatever part of your meetings concerns you most right now. As you make changes, we feel sure you'll find yourself using this book more and more every week, whether to polish your skills or to find new topics and new ways to use traditional topics to increase the knowledge, sharpen the skills and influence the attitudes of your salespeople.

CHAPTER 1

Concept of sales meeting

WHAT IS A SALES MEETING?

In the real estate business, a sales meeting is a gathering of management and salespeople where information is exchanged, training is given, problems are discussed or ideas are explored, any one or all of which can lead to improved sales performance.

Sales meetings are common in real estate firms of all sizes, ranging from the majority of companies with ten or fewer salespeople to multi-office firms where branches meet individually on a regular basis and come together in branch or all-company meetings from time to time. Even one-man firms meet in peer groups to discuss problems and opportunities in a given market.

All these meetings lead to what in modern marketing terminology is called synergism, defined by Webster as "cooperative action of separate agencies (people) such that the total effect is greater than the sum of the individuals working independently."

WHY HAVE SALES MEETINGS?

Why indeed? There are dozens of times each week when a real estate sales manager sits down with individual salespeople to counsel them on particular problems. On the other hand, there

1

are experienced, skillful, motivated salespeople who go their own way, doing a fine job for themselves and for the company, seldom seeming to need counsel or to share the creativity of others. But there are times when the neophyte, the experienced and all the others in between need to be brought together for a free exchange of ideas and information, to explore problems and to use the combined knowledge and creativity of the group for the benefit of all. *That's why sales meetings are held.* And when they're good, that's what they accomplish.

In good sales meetings experienced, skillful salespeople undergird newer ones while the latter look at old problems with fresh eyes, unrestrained by the limitations of tradition and thus are often able to offer fresh new solutions. (If they don't know it can't be done, maybe it can!) When these things happen, everybody benefits.

There's another basic reason for having sales meetings. Man is by nature a social species, needing to share common bonds in a face-to-face setting, whether at work or play. Just as in earlier times the tribal council discussed how to cope with daily challenges, today's business people have a very human need to get together. Management that is aware of this need can plan the kind of sales meetings where everyone participates. When this occurs, the anticipation of participation and the benefit to be gained have a good effect on meeting attendance. All the memos, newsletters, bulletin boards, books, magazines and tape recordings in the world cannot replace the stimulation and enthusiasm generated in a lively sales meeting.

GETTING PEOPLE TO ATTEND

Getting salespeople to attend meetings is often a problem, especially if they have an independent contractor relationship with the broker. (This topic is treated more fully in *Real Estate Office Management.*[1]) Very few real estate salespeople are *employed* by brokers in the traditional sense—i.e., paid a salary. When they are, the broker may require them to attend the meetings. But if they are *independent contractors* they cannot be told to come. They tell *you* whether or not your meetings have value by their presence or absence. The Yes men always come. Take your cue from the negative ones whose "independence" includes not coming. Make it your personal (but unstated) goal to get them to attend. When they come, you'll know you've scored.

Meetings must be so worthwhile your salespeople will want to come voluntarily. They are spending their own time (translated "money") and expect to get something useful (ways to make more money) in return. The "something useful" can be as diverse as market information, new skills, suggestions for handling a difficult listing or sale—in fact, anything a manager can think of to improve the knowledge, skills and attitudes of his people.

ECONOMICS OF SALES MEETINGS

Sales meetings are a costly way to spend people's time. The cost figures may not appear in the budget and they may never have occurred to management. Thought of in the context of dollar cost to salespeople, sales meetings held once a week for ten salespeople whose incomes average $15,000 a year cost them more than $4250 a year in time alone. Add to that figure the cost of the manager's time and the cost edges up toward $5500. (These figures are perhaps too modest. Adjust them to fit your operation.)

If the advertising budget for one office runs $5000 a year (a hypothetical figure), a broker is likely to plan that expenditure with care, knowing in advance what he expects it to do for the business and measuring its effectiveness after the money is spent. Sales meeting cost/effectiveness ought to be measured in the same way.

Looking at sales meetings in this way can help management spot the wasteful traditions built into the system and do something to change them. Keeping an eye on the cost/effectiveness of sales meetings can also alert a manager to whether he's been using sales meetings as a weekly treatment for his ego; and it will help turn him around to becoming a manager who carries water for his people so they can get on with their jobs so everybody makes more money. And it can help management spot the phonies who cater to them with Yes answers and optimistic predictions instead of realistic goals and who generally put forth their greatest effort to nurture the boss' tender ego. That's no help to the bottom line of a real estate business.

TWO IMPORTANT QUESTIONS

In hard dollars and cents figures, are sales meetings achieving the results you want, both for the benefit of the sales staff and the company?

Have you ever studied exactly what the company's objectives are and the priorities within the objectives for its sales meeting program?

In thinking about the objectives to be set for sales meetings and what can be planned to provide the best stimuli for the majority of your sales staff, it is well to keep in mind something called Pareto's Principle[2] or the 80/20 rule. The rules goes something like this:

If all items are arranged in order of value, 80 percent of the value would come from only 20 percent of the items, while the remaining 20 percent of the value would come from 80 percent of the items.

Adapting this principle to real estate selling, 80 percent of a firm's volume is accounted for by 20 percent of the sales staff; the remaining 20 percent of sales are produced by 80 percent of the staff.

Expressed in individual activities, 20 percent of a person's activities account for 80 percent of the value of all his activities. This means that the remaining 80 percent of his activities account for 20 percent of his effort value, the busy work he deludes himself into doing each day.

Your challenge is to stimulate the sales staff to learn to concentrate on the 20 percent activities with the high value.

WHO SETS OBJECTIVES?

You do, if you're the manager or owner of a single office operation. This is the size and situation of approximately 75 percent of the real estate brokerage operations in the United States today: a single owner, one-office operation with ten or fewer salespeople.

The likelihood is great that the owner is also active in selling. He knows what the daily problems are, takes the pulse of the market as it signals change and knows what he wants to do and how he wants to do it. If he doesn't sell and his sales staff is small enough, he has enough time to learn what he needs to know in order to set objectives.

In larger organizations the method of setting objectives is more complicated. The general sales manager and the president meet to discuss and agree on where the emphasis should be for the coming week for the company as a whole. (It could be listings, need of buyers, change in advertising emphasis or methods, telephone techniques or telephone canvassing and so on.)

The determination made, that objective becomes the basis of the manager's meeting, where branch office managers meet to report on activities in their area and discuss with management what the direction of that week's sales meetings should be. Such an arrangement gives *direction* to the sales meetings in individual offices but it is still the responsibility of the local manager to adapt that direction to the needs of his particular office. For example, one office may be heavy on listings because it's a "transfer town" with continuing turnover in ownership; another office may be in an older, more static area where the problem is getting listings because so few properties come on the market. If listings are the major emphasis with this company, the sales meetings for the two offices would have quite different agendas. But the *company* objective remains the same for both.

There is a danger in local offices wanting to plug in special items at meetings, resulting in the loss of the primary objective. The general sales manager keeps tabs on developments of this sort by having each office submit its meeting agendas.

THE COMPANY OBJECTIVE

Management's main, continuing objective is to build an organization which is profitable and can withstand the peaks and valleys of the local market and the general economy. Everything done is bent in this direction, whether it be recruiting salespeople, training and then retaining them, developing budgets, choosing office sites, deciding to expand the business or to hold to its present size, or determining what kinds of outside services and counsel are needed and where to find them.

SALES MEETING OBJECTIVES

While objectives for sales meetings might include one or more of those just mentioned, most of the time they are focused on providing help for the immediate job—getting listings and making sales.

Sales meeting objectives combine what you want for the business (profit) with what salespeople want (good income). Stated another way, sales meeting objectives are set to increase the knowledge and skills and to improve the attitude of the sales staff so they will do something they've not been doing or so they stop doing what they have been doing wrong—in short, to make a behavioral change.

WHY SET OBJECTIVES?

Objectives that are well thought out can be used to convert company or staff needs to meeting topics. Objectives should be organized so you can state them to the group at the beginning of a meeting, guide the meeting action toward achieving the objective and then, at the end of the session, summarize what's been done. Objectives organized and used in this way enable you to close the meeting on an upbeat note, avoiding having it taper off to a ragged ending where nobody quite knows what happened or why or whether anything happened at all.

Independent contractors can't be told to come to meetings. Once there (whether employees *or* independent contractors), you can't make them listen. But when the staff knows their reward for attending will be knowledge or a skill they can put to work as soon as the meeting ends, they'll make it a point to be there. Some companies prepare a series of meeting topics and distribute them to the sales staff once a month along with suggested reading topics and sources. The staff, guided by notices and advance preparation, comes ready to discuss the assigned topic and ask questions that relate to it. This practice usually results in greater participation of the entire staff in the meeting.

OBJECTIVES SUGGEST TOPICS

Developments within the firm may suggest the time is right to present a new sales concept. A shortage of listings may indicate it's time to retrain the staff on listing techniques so more of the good ones come to your firm. If the local market is in a slump a refresher course in basic selling skills may keep the company ahead of competition. News of a new industry coming to the area may lead to a discussion on how the firm can zero in on the possible transferees the move promises. Sales training literature may suggest a film on real estate sales psychology everyone would benefit by seeing. The list of potential topics is limited only by your imagination and the framework of your objectives.

KINDS OF SALES MEETINGS

Some meetings will involve the entire staff; others may be planned to help only those with particular problems; still others are set up for the top producers in the firm. The key is to have several kinds of meetings—some to share information, some for problem solving and still others to focus on either short- or long-range planning and training or to hear outside speakers.

As people associate with one another under conditions of equality, the importance of effective communication grows. In a real estate office this means not only daily communication as the sales staff pursues their goals but also the more structured communication necessary to group sessions. There is valuable information to share in sales meetings as well as a need to discuss differences and solve problems in a setting where valid judgment is the determinant and not where the fellow who speaks loudest and longest "wins."

Over a period of time a sales meeting plan should include three important elements: knowledge, skills and attitudes. An exhaustive list of possible topics (see Appendix A) is presented under these headings. Such a plan will counter the common complaint of salespeople: *"We spend* (translate *'give') all that time and don't really get anything useful out of the meetings."*

Eight questions help in getting started. The first four are asked by salespeople:

What's it about?
What's in it for me?
Can I do it?
How much time will it take from my day?

Management also has four questions:

What's the objective for this meeting?
What's in it for the firm and for the staff?
Are they prepared to accomplish it?
How can I lead the group toward achieving it?

Each one of these questions is vital to a good sales meeting program, from preliminary planning to the final follow-up, and they are adaptable to almost any kind of meeting.

AVOID TRADITION

Real estate, like other industries, clings to some time-honored but often hoary traditions. Like the one that implies that a broker should have a sales meeting every week whether he is prepared for it or not. Out of such a tradition comes the perhaps apocryphal story of the sales manager who mutters to himself as he opens the office door the morning of the weekly sales meeting, "What in the world will I talk to them about today?"

In the modern real estate brokerage offices that tradition and the people who ran such impromptu weekly sessions have gone the way of the dodo bird. Today's skillful broker knows what his objectives are and what the needs and wants of his salespeople are; and he learns how to combine them into forceful, productive sales meetings that benefit everyone who attends. With the wealth of meeting topics and communication techniques available, you can make your sales meetings so informative and helpful that everyone eligible to attend will make it a point to be there.

The frequency of meetings is not as important as the content. Attendance by every salesperson is not necessarily related to the success of a meeting or the success of the business. What is important is that each meeting have an objective that will serve both you and your people, giving everyone a degree of self-renewal and stimulation they can put to work to their immediate and/or long-range benefit.

EACH SITUATION IS UNIQUE

There are guidelines here to consult in deciding what sales
meetings can do and how to change some old practices and begin
to develop new ones. There is no single "right way" to plan and
conduct sales meetings. Solutions to real estate brokerage
problems are not portable. Your problems could be almost identical to or they may be vastly different from the broker down the
street. Whatever the case, do things your own way. The last
thing to do is to copy somebody else.

A strong sense of self is an attribute in developing a plan for
sales meetings. Staying power is important because change will
be slow in coming and there are always people around the place
who resist change despite their expressed restiveness with the
status quo.

On the other hand, a plan for sales meetings is likely to result
in your giving more consideration to the needs and creativity of
the sales staff, listening to them and their ideas in a receptive
mood, alert to their need to contribute whatever ideas they have
and giving them courage to speak up in meetings or to submit
their ideas privately. Anything done to open up genuine communication with salespeople will pay immense dividends. If you
listen to them, really listen, they're likely to listen more attentively to you.

TOTAL PARTICIPATION IMPORTANT

Everyone invited to attend sales meetings should be encouraged
to participate, whether by joining in a discussion, offering an
opinion or suggesting a new, original idea. Whether or not every
person participates every time is not the point. Rather, it is that
anyone asked to give time to the meeting should feel he is a
member of the team, to be "in the game" and not restricted to
being "on the bench."

The skillful leader also moves to another level of participation
as the need or opportunity arises: he may become the expert or
simply try to be helpful. When the leadership role is clearly
defined and the leader is skillful in shifting to give an expert
opinion when sought or is receptive to the ideas offered by sub-
ordinates, chances for the meeting's success are very greatly
enhanced.

Ambivalence in leadership and forcing management's ideas on
the group to the exclusion of considering others' results in a
general feeling of antagonism by salespeople toward the whole
concept of sales meetings.

SALESPEOPLE'S COMPLAINTS

A random sampling of salespeople's complaints about how meetings go in their organization revealed several that were mentioned enough to suggest they are fairly common. We list them here with the thought that you may recognize some, may not be aware of others but will want to keep them in mind as you read this book, adding those heard around your own place. We'll mention them again on occasion, setting them up as "Complaint: . . ."in sections of the book dealing with the particular complaint.

"We hold so many meetings around here there's not enough time left to do the job."

"The broker (or sales manager) does almost all the talking."

"If you're new to real estate, your speculations and suggestions are not valued. And quite often you're not encouraged to contribute them."

"The meeting gets off the track and time is wasted in unrelated chit-chat."

"The broker ramrods his decisions through without asking for our reactions, much less welcoming our opinions and ideas."

"One person is allowed to dominate the meeting whenever the broker asks for staff opinions or ideas."

"There's never a chance to introduce something we want to talk about."

"We never start on time, never get out on time."

"Meetings drag on after the real business has been handled."

"We've never been asked our opinion of sales meetings. We'd like to be able to do this anonymously."

MANAGEMENT'S COMPLAINTS

You have complaints, too. They are just as valid as your salespeople's. The difference lies in the fact that it's up to you to do something about both.

Salespeople's complaints may look like a forbidding list. Don't let it get you down. But try not to think of them in the context of retribution. List them and see how many of yours "match" theirs: *their not listening to you, starting random conversations that develop into time wasters and take you all off the main target; or their failing to respond when you ask for opinions and ideas.*

Suggestions for controlling problem situations in a positive way are in the chapter on Conducting the Meeting; Logistics has hints for different meeting places or for making occasional changes in the physical arrangement of a meeting room; the chapter on Preparation shows how advance work saves everybody's time; and the suggestions in Meeting Topics will provide ideas for fresh, new subjects to be discussed and some new ways to treat time-worn topics.

Stress the positive. Be aware of problems and complaints but use them only in an ancillary way. Focus thinking and preparation on the positive objectives of meetings. Negatives won't disappear but neither will they dominate thinking. The main responsibility is to put on a good meeting.

Because a firm's success is tied directly to the success of its people, the needs of both are logical concerns. The individual salesperson's needs and wants ought to be known and the meetings' objectives geared to helping fill those needs. The content of every meeting should have value for both management and staff. Sometimes the value will be evident, at other times more subtle but nonetheless there.

ELEMENTS OF THE BUSINESS

Real estate selling consists of two elements: people and properties. They are the source of objectives for every meeting. Both people and properties lead to the bottom line of the business.

People

First, people. You and "them." Salespeople. You need good salespeople as much as they need you. Maybe more. After all, there's always the office down the street waiting to attract the most productive people. But these are the very ones *you* need most.

It is an old saw in the real estate industry that most of the volume is produced by very few people. If this is true, you'll want to provide different sales helps, even different meetings for the top producers. Their needs and wants (and yours in relation to them) are very different than the needs and wants of the others.

People who acquire the combined skills needed for selling real estate can go on to sell almost any other product or service, but they seldom do. Where else can they find a career with the challenges *and* the freedoms found in real estate?

The second "people" element is management—your concern for the financial success of the business and that it fill the personal needs and wants of your salespeople.

There is a third "people" element in real estate, of course, the people whose properties the firm wants to list and service and the people who will buy those properties. This "people" element is a constant consideration. It *is* a vital element of every sales meeting plan.

Properties

The second element in real estate sales is properties. Properties are the merchandise of the real estate brokerage business.

Selling real estate differs from selling raw materials or manufactured goods produced or processed by the seller. Real estate has been produced by someone else (from raw land to residences, industrial and commercial buildings), the quality of which is beyond the broker's control. Thus, real estate salespeople are selling somebody else's goods.

Sales meeting objectives will naturally include a focus on the merchandise salespeople will have to sell—what it is, where it is, how to get it and how to sell it. This type of objective is why salespeople *think* they come to sales meetings. But it isn't, really. Actually, they come *first* because of their hierarchy of needs and *then* to learn more about the merchandise and how they must sell their services in order to satisfy those needs.

PEOPLE'S NEEDS

In this computer age of "do not fold, spindle or mutilate," people are anxious to be treated like human beings. Ever since the dawn of the industrial revolution in 1760 at Huddersfield, England, business has been moving away from an awareness of human needs. This is as true in real estate as in any other industry, but it ought to be less true than it is. We are trying to train real estate salespeople to understand human needs and to listen to and watch for all the signals that reveal the things property sellers and buyers want. An understanding of people, like charity, should begin at home—right in every brokerage office. Good modern management studies its staff's needs as thoroughly as its customers'.

What are salespeople's needs? Basically, the same as yours. It's important for you to understand salespeople's needs in order to set workable objectives. The better you know what is motivating them *at the moment*, the better you can communicate with them.

MASLOW'S HIERARCHY

Years ago the late Dr. Abraham Maslow, father of humanist psychology, developed what he called "the hierarchy of human needs." It has come to be accepted as practical knowledge for management people. Maslow portrayed it graphically in a pyramid divided into five levels, each representing an area of human need.[3]

Starting at the base of the pyramid and proceeding upward, human needs are physiological (food, shelter, air), security (protection from present and future danger), social (a sense of belonging, acceptance and respect from one's fellows), ego (self-esteem and status) and, finally self-actualization (development, growth and creativity).

These are salespeople's needs. They are also management's needs. They are, in fact, the needs of everyone. When one level of need is satisfied, another comes into focus and determines where the individual's energy is expended. The lowest unmet need has the most influence on the individual. All five may at some time or other represent a need for money in hand, at other times they may have no connection with money per se (especially the top three levels of needs). But all five relate to where and how we all earn our living. The relationship may be as direct (physiological) as the amount of commissions earned by salespeople or the bottom line of the annual profit and loss statement for the owners. Or it may be as indirect as salespeople wanting to work for a firm because of its prestige and reputation in the community, or a broker wanting a certain salesperson to affiliate with him because he's "top drawer" in town (ego) and can acquire listings (security) by virtue of his personal and business contacts as well as his selling skills.

An examination of the five levels of needs will reveal logical ways for every one of them to be satisfied in a real estate career. Take time to identify your own hierarchy of needs, using the inventory below or one you prepare yourself, identifying needs at each level. Once you've done this, get individual salespeople to do the same. Beyond giving a better understanding of everybody's needs, it will be a help to you in deciding the kinds of meetings to have.

You can ascertain your people's needs by getting them to answer the questions in the motivation inventory on page 14, adapted from one prepared by Dr. Philip R. Harris,[4] nationally known management psychologist. This inventory reflects the basic needs recognized in the Maslow hierarchy, adapted to real estate salespeople. You may wish to add other questions.

Needs are listed here in the order of their importance on the Maslow hierarchy. Though people move up and down from survival to actualization, their needs at a given time may be concentrated in one area or may cover several. Also, people in different age groups tend to have different needs. When you get to know what motivates your people you will be able to plan sales meetings that encourage them to perform better.

Maslow Hierarchy of Needs*

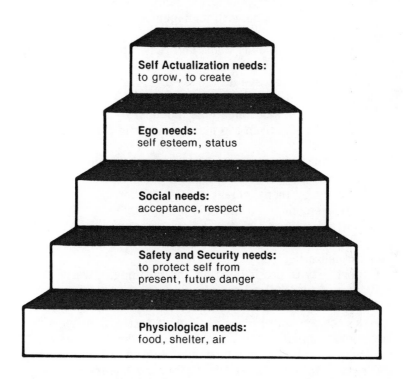

*Adapted from *Motivation and Personality*, 2nd edition, 1970, by permission of Harper & Row, publishers.

Motivation Inventory

Physiological needs
  Assurance of a good income
  Good working conditions
  Vacations and holidays free
  Good living standard for my family
Security
  Good commission rate
  Company goals I understand and agree with
  Regular interviews with management so I know how I'm doing
  Written policy and procedures manual
  Good communications with management
Belonging
  Knowledge of company plans and, when practical, some part
    in formulating them
  Praise when I deserve it
  Cooperative fellow salespeople
  Participation in sales meetings (not just by attending)
  Occasional visits from top management (in a large firm)
Esteem
  Plan for increasing income as my sales improve
  Sense that my work is important
  Treatment by management as a professional
  Encouragement to do the best job possible
  Opportunity to gain status in the company
  Opportunity for creativity
Self Actualization
  Opportunity to do challenging and meaningful work
  Chances for self-development and improvement
  Opportunity to experience sense of accomplishment

Ask each person to place an X next to the five items he believes most important self-motivators in doing his work, then
to place a √ by the five next most important items. Tabulate
the results to learn what the motivating factors are for your
people. This information is a valuable guide in planning sales
meeting objectives tailored to the needs of your staff. It is basic
and useful regardless of the kind of meeting you are planning.
Just as important, it will help you deal with each person on a
one-to-one basis more productively.

---

1. *Real Estate Office Management: People, Functions, Systems*, Chapter 9.
2. Vilfredo Pareto, Italian economist 1848-1923.
3. For a fuller explanation, see *Real Estate Office Management: People, Functions, Systems*, Chapter 1.
4. Dr. Harris, *Sales Meeting Magazine*, December, 1974.

CHAPTER 2

Kinds of sales meetings

Peter Drucker, the economist famed for his Management by Objectives concept, warns that "so much of what we call management consists in making it difficult for people to work." A sales manager's major challenge in the real estate business today is to help his sales staff make admittedly difficult work easier to do. You accomplish this by giving individual attention to staff members and by planning and conducting meaty, helpful sales meetings. It's not easy to do. In the words of Douglas S. Sherwin, Executive Vice President of Phillips Products Co. in a recent article "Management *of* Objectives" in *Harvard Business Review*,[1] "Every business is in tension between the need to get the routine operations of the day done and the need to bring about the changes that will improve the business for tomorrow."

What kinds of sales meetings can you plan, heeding Drucker's warning and avoiding at least some of the tension Sherwin mentions?

A MANAGER LOOKS AT HIS PAST

People with a reputation for good sales meetings point out that it's important to remember one's own reflexes from early days in the business. Ask yourself these questions.

15

How did I feel during my first sales meeting?
Was I afraid? Of what? Of whom? Why?
Was I bored? Why?
Was I frustrated? Why?
What happened in those early days to stimulate my interest?
In my experience as a salesperson which manager had the best
    meetings? Why?

With those questions and their answers firmly in mind, you then ask what you can do to help the salespeople—experienced or newcomers—achieve whatever self-motivation they need.

TWO TYPES OF MEETINGS

Sales meetings are generally divided into two types: educational and inspirational. A single meeting can be both educational and inspirational, whether consciously planned that way or not. Each type gives a chance to develop the all-important team concept.

Some firms deliberately alternate meeting types, having educational sessions one week, inspirational the next. Some carefully combine the two because they believe the staff has such a diversity of needs to be satisfied and every person should get some help at every meeting.

With the right emphasis and skillful direction, a sales manager can effectively shape his staff and reinforce it on a weekly basis. Sales meetings offer the ideal vehicle to promote the individual's understanding that his aims are part of and important to the aims of the others and the company as a whole, showing how each can contribute to the success of the others.

FIVE MEETING STYLES

Sales meetings can be separated into five general styles. Every office with more than one salesperson is probably familiar with them.

Shared information
Discussion
Training
Company plans
Brainstorming

All these styles can provide each salesperson with something he can put to work five minutes after he leaves a meeting—the best "prize" management can give him to reward his attendance and participation.

Shared information

Perhaps more real estate meeting hours are spent sharing sales and listing information than on any other single topic. Shared information includes things like reviewing new listings, changes in current listings, impending expiration of current listings, news of new buyers and their needs and wants. Shared information also reaches beyond the merchandise of real estate. It can include the latest mortgage money sources, any changes in government regulation and legislation (from local to federal) and new developments in local industry and business that may affect the firm's business or local market conditions.

In general, information sharing ought to include everything that's "hard news" and beyond the stages of rumor. Even rumors and "what if" discussions can often be developed into useful information under the guidance of a skilled sales manager.

In a shared information meeting, salespeople have their chance to inform the staff of new listings, giving them the dual opportunity to rehearse what they'll say in response to inquiries (both from other brokers and from prospects). Then if the property has been visited by the staff, other members can be asked what impressed them most about it. This often results in better advertising and promotion of the property.

Information sharing of this sort is the most traditional part of real estate sales meetings. But don't be restricted by what's been done. Shake it up, look it over and see if there isn't a new approach that could *make it new*.

Discussion

Here's where everybody ought to be brought into the act. Problems come in all sizes and shapes, some familiar and some brand new. Look for ways to let salespeople air their problems as well as new ways to share company concerns with them. When you succeed in doing this, everybody gets a lift from the meeting.

Open discussions can be very hard for a manager accustomed to dominating the scene. He owns or manages the business, so why shouldn't he have the answers? Well, he doesn't or he wouldn't be airing problems to the group, would he? A company problem is the sales staff's problem, too. Even if your solution proves to be the final, accepted one, let others help reach that decision. Sales meetings are for build-ups, not put-downs. Your role, basically, is to keep the discussion from getting off target.

Listen to everybody else's suggestions first. Why? Because that's the only way management hears from a good many people. Save for a few of the strongest characters, if a manager puts his solutions first the others will feel it's all terribly pat, so why should they bother to even think about it much less speak up? It may be hard at first, but try going around the group, asking for each person's ideas or opinions. It's a fine way to encourage courage in the shy and to help prevent the discussion being dominated by the most vocal people.

Training

Whether the company has a separate training program or not, some training or retraining during sales meetings is a part of almost every broker's sales meeting program. Such training can take the form of polishing old skills when the staff is getting a bit rusty or it can introduce new skills as the local market presents new opportunities. A new concept in private housing or the development of a major corporate relocation operation are two training opportunities that come to mind.

Company plans

Company plans offer exciting possibilities for sales meetings but have been little used by many firms.

Some brokers say these meetings include everything from a review of the company policy and procedures manual (and the possible need for revisions) to an examination and discussion of the coming year's advertising plan and budget.

If, for example, salespeople are told how much is budgeted for classified ads in the next year and they agree to it, they have little recourse to come back later and say not enough is being spent on weekly classified when they happen to be in a sales slump.

Some firms report they never really developed a company policy until the manager challenged himself by putting the subject on a sales meeting agenda. How you do this is important. Don't ever get in a position where you lose control of things that are your prerogative or where salespeople begin to think they are making the decisions around the place.

Design your plan or policy or procedure, then present it to the group as a benefit to them as well as to the firm. When you sell benefits you excite them and enlist their cooperation. But if you ram it down their throats it has the opposite effect.

When a policy has to be discussed and maybe defended, it is more likely to have been given careful thought. And when the salespeople discuss the firm's policy and procedures in a sales meeting they can and often do go out on the street afterward and boast about what a great firm they're affiliated with. As they talk it up around town, word gets around and the firm enjoys growing prestige in the business community.

Another benefit to discussing company plans in sales meetings is that it can generate ideas for adding new services. Real estate is undergoing drastic change. If the firm wants to be out in front leading the pack in the local market, now's the time to start finding out what other creative, aggressive brokers around the country are doing, then determine how some of their ideas and programs fit the local market and business conditions.

What services are needed in the market that relate to *serving* real estate customers that no one else has offered? For example, what about the commercial housecleaning service being provided in many areas of the country by firms that do one-time clean up jobs in everything from private residences to office buildings to hospitals and industrial plants? One such firm reports that this service influenced the sale of a property that had been on the market far longer than it would have had it been cleaned up earlier.

More and more brokers are working up lists of reliable firms for both minor and major renovation and restoration services as well as for carpeting, wallpapering and other interior design work. Perhaps you'll want to have a brainstorming session on the subject.

Brainstorming

Brainstorming offers a fine way to generate total participation of the sales staff in truly creative thinking. It can be a brief, spontaneous session like using the "break" point in a film or cassette for two or three minutes; or it can be the main emphasis of a meeting with the session lasting as much as a half hour.

Whole books have been written on the subject, among them Charles H. Clark's *Brainstorming,*[2] which has been the bible of the process for close to two decades. Clark writes, "The secret of a good brainstorming session, like a good proposal of marriage, is spontaneity. And the secret of such spontaneity, of course, is good planning."

Four rules

Brainstorming techniques are based on four rules, established by Alex Osborn, in *Applied Imagination.*[3]

Criticism is ruled out. *Adverse judgment of ideas must be withheld until later.*

"Free-wheeling" is welcomed. *The wilder the idea, the better; it is easier to tame down than to think up.*

Quantity is wanted. *The greater the number of ideas, the more the likelihood of winners.*

Combination and Improvement are sought. *In addition to contributing ideas of their own, participants should suggest how ideas of others can be turned into* better *ideas; or how two or more ideas can be joined into still another idea.*

Clark says further, "Good planning does not mean establishing a forbidding atmosphere; in fact, everything should be done to avoid that. It does mean quiet planning that will make the session relaxed, a success. If you are to be the brainstorm leader, do your job well, but be unobtrusive. Don't tell everyone how much you've done, how hard you've worked. Brainstorming is a team effort. Don't try to take the credit. You'll get enough if the group comes up with good ideas, but like a good team captain, stay in the background yourself."

Absolute freedom to offer any idea as quickly as it comes to mind is the real secret of success in brainstorming. It's a cardinal principle *never to stop and criticize* anything that's been offered. If, for example, you're brainstorming on a new slogan for the company and somebody comes up with a suggestion that your firm might consider unethical, write it down anyway. It will not last beyond the critiquing stage which comes later, having either died of inattention or been discarded *by the group.* If you stop to criticize or tell why something isn't ethical or won't work, you've killed the brainstorming right then and there. Everyone in the room will be restricted, fearing the next thing *they* say may be rejected.

Ways to keep it going

If and when the session slows down or gets off the track, you can prime the flow of ideas by contributing some of your own ideas, but more importantly, you should be prepared to ask idea-spurring questions.

What other ideas does this suggest?
What else is like this?
Should we add to this?
Does this suggest new uses for the old slogan?
Are the words attention-getting?
Should we turn it backward?
What to subtract? Eliminate? Add?

You can sometimes stimulate the flow of ideas by the use of an egg-timer to measure a three-minute drive for ideas. This could be used as the wind-up for the session, the means of pulling out those final ideas that might otherwise be lost if the meeting is allowed to run down.

You might decide to brainstorm to get ideas on how to move your firm up into top place in the local REALTOR® community. Here's one way to do it.

Write down on a chalkboard or easel the names of three real estate firms in the area. One will be topnotch, one mediocre and one you consider the bottom of the list. Say not a word about any of the three. Pass out sheets of paper to the salespeople, asking each to write down the firm names and what comes to mind about them. Collect the papers. Discuss which firm they want to be like. Now ask them to brainstorm ideas for making their firm more like the best one in town. They'll very likely repeat the things they've already written about the top firm. They will also add others. Write down every one.

In the critique stage, after all the ideas have been written down, select the ones most readily possible, the ones most difficult and the ones that may have to wait awhile. Out of one brainstorming session you've got quite a list of ideas, you've got the whole staff thinking *toward* making the firm better and you've involved everybody in the room in a creative exercise.

Osborn comments that one by-product of brainstorm is the enjoyment experienced by those who participate. One person said, "I had a wonderful time. At the end I felt exhilarated; but an hour later I felt tired. It is a fatiguing experience, and yet it's fun. The usual conference is far less tiring. It's about the same difference as between golf and tennis. In golf, you just amble along, but in tennis, you sweat. I like strenuous effort—that's why I enjoy brainstorming."

A salesperson's image quiz is another good brainstorming idea. List on the chalkboard or easel all the ways they want to impress sellers and buyers; then ask each person to rate himself from one to ten, ten being tops.

Questions could include the following, but they should be the salespeople's, not management's.

How do I dress?
How do I speak?
What is my attitude?
How do I use my time?
Do I work to improve my professionalism?
Do I eat right and get proper rest?
Do I keep myself in good physical shape?
Do I work to broaden my acquaintance in the community?

Ten questions ought to be enough. Salespeople will usually come up with that many in less than a minute. Management shouldn't offer any except as a last resort.

WHO PARTICIPATES IN SALES MEETINGS?

You, the manager or owner, and your salespeople usually constitute the meeting group. Occasionally, in some firms, a member of the office staff is included. Now and then outside speakers are invited to speak about or discuss with the staff their specialty.

There is much difference of opinion about including people from the office staff in sales meetings. Some firms make it a regular practice, others never do it. Those who favor the practice say it's a fine way to save time (yours) and keep communications open between the office staff and the salespeople. For example, if a new listing promotion is about to start and it will require new records from the salespeople, you'll save time by telling them all about it at once and making sure both the sales and the office staff understand what's required and why.

Other brokers feel it's best to keep the secretary/bookkeeper/receptionist out of sales meetings. In most cases these managers prefer to be the conduit for information and complaints between the office and selling staff.

Outside speakers can bring the staff useful information and guidance relating to their field of work. For example, a company's legal counsel can explain the elements of an independent contractor relationship, how it works and why it's important for every salesperson to understand fully all its implications; an accountant could be invited to discuss the tax advantages of the salespeople's independent contractor relationship, independent retirement plans and other matters germane to their income tax situation; an officer from a local mortgage company or the bank with which the firm does business could discuss availability of funds; a public official can explain zoning, tax rates and other topics that influence property values and community development; administrators of public institutions (libraries, hospitals, schools) can explain their service and facilities and how they add to the livability of the market the firm serves. Real estate salespeople are important to every one of these specialists (and they are important to the salespeople) for they are in the front line, selling the community as a good place to live and/or conduct business or locate an industry. Such a list goes on and on, limited only by the sales manager's imagination and suggestions gleaned from the staff.

Outside speakers bring other benefits

In addition to being flattered to be asked to participate in your sales meeting, most outsiders enjoy benefits to their own business by learning more about yours. For example, a savings and loan executive said his firm did a much better job in handling settlements after he'd talked to a brokerage sales meeting. Why? How? Because, as he prepared his presentation for the real estate group, he discovered how his firm could be doing things differently and better to the mutual benefit of customers, REALTORS® and his own institution.

Another plus relating to outside speakers is that they have a nice, warm feeling about being included in your firm's meetings and go away from a well-conducted meeting as a real missionary for you. It's a public relations benefit you couldn't ever buy or contract for.

Sales meetings without management people or their representative present are likened to a ship without a rudder. Whether "management" is the owner, the general manager or the sales or branch manager, every meeting needs someone with the knowledge and authority to answer questions and to control the direction of the meeting. Even if management's representative has to say "I don't know, but I'll find out and get back to you," at least that person has access to someone who has the answer or the power to make a decision.

Some large firms with a number of branch operations arrange for managers to take another's meeting occasionally. They report this practice broadens the outlook of the managers involved, helping them see beyond their own branch operation. Another positive result is that the salespeople appreciate their own manager more when he comes back to the next meeting.

Every rule has its exceptions. One fairly common exception to the above rule is when a salesperson develops an exciting new concept of putting together a selling package or has found a solution to a problem that's bugged the less experienced staff; then the manager invites that salesperson to present his concept or solution to the group. The manager may wish to sit in on the meeting or he may have another commitment that takes him away from the group entirely. If possible, he is on hand to introduce the person in charge and state the objective of the meeting to the group. That "sets up" the speaker with management's blessing and gives everyone the challenge of learning from a peer. And without actually being mentioned, the practice suggests to the rest of the staff that if one of them comes up with something equally new and worthwhile the moment of glory awaits him, too.

Among the changes in sales meeting concepts over the years is the move away from the old belief that everybody has to be at every sales meeting and that the lack of a full house is a personal slur against management.

HOW OFTEN SHOULD SALES MEETINGS BE HELD?

The frequency of your sales meetings depends on your objectives
for them. In a new office, daily meetings are not out of the ordi-
nary. They're important as the staff begins working together,
getting acquainted with each other and the market place and
encountering situations that require both discussion with and
decisions from management.

Well-established offices alter their meeting schedules to
handle special situations. For example, if you've just announced
a new campaign for listings and are using both radio and tele-
vision to get the message to the public about some basic changes
in your services and commissions, you'll likely want to meet
every day or every other day for awhile. The new program will
bring responses to the whole sales staff that everyone ought to
know about. As manager you can help the staff short-circuit
some developing problems if you know about them in time even
though this might necessitate a change from what might otherwise be a once-a-week schedule for a well-established firm.

As a general rule, however, sales meetings are scheduled once
a week in individual offices; monthly or quarterly with combined
staffs and, in some cases, semi-annually or annually for participation of the firm's entire staff.

ARE ALL YOUR SALES MEETINGS NECESSARY?

(Complaint: *We hold so many meetings around here there's not
enough time left to do the job.*)

During the transportation crisis of World War II the U.S.
government, in an effort to relieve overcrowded trains and
planes and the profligate use of scarce gasoline supplies, coined
the phrase "Is this trip necessary?" It became the butt of jokes,
the object of cartoonists' skills, but it was on the lips of the
masses and helped cut down on unnecessary travel.

Sales managers today are asking themselves a similar question: Is this meeting necessary? Should we meet every week? Is
there some better way to handle routine matters we've been
dealing with at sales meetings? Could we have several different
kinds of meetings, some of which might not involve the whole
staff?

What are sales meetings supposed to accomplish that could not
be done in some other way? Information can be shared in a group
that might be missed if you depend on people to read a bulletin
board or if you attempt to convey it on a one-to-one basis with
each salesperson. And, as the information is shared, it often
stimulates a discussion or exchange of ideas that would be

missed entirely in a non-group setting. This form of self-renewal and stimulation is necessary to everyone.

WHEN *NOT* TO HAVE MEETINGS

If there is no valid reason for a meeting, don't have it just to sustain the weekly habit. Let salespeople get out and do their job rather than warm chairs back at the office. When they understand that every meeting called has a legitimate objective and that they can each take something worthwhile from every meeting, attendance will improve.

Look at it this way: Suppose routine matters involving individual salespeople were discussed by having nine salespeople each spend five minutes with the manager. That combined time (manager and salespeople's) totals one and one-half hours. If the whole group is called into a meeting and spends the same amount of time listening to routine reports the total time spent is multiplied by ten. Those hours might be used more profitably by the salespeople in the pursuit of business. It's a judgment management must make.

A further advantage to the one-on-one exchange is that spending just five minutes alone with each person allows both the manager and the salesperson to bring up individual problems and concerns that may not belong in a sales meeting. Personal attention of this sort is needed by every salesperson, regardless of his production level. Any matters that should be discussed with the entire staff as a result of these personal conferences can go on the agenda for the next general sales meeting.

HAVE A "SALESPERSON'S HOUR"

One very successful commercial investment broker established "the salesperson's hour." His sales manager is available every weekday morning from 8:30 to 9:30 to help with salespeople's problems. Individual problems may not be brought up during sales meeting time. The broker reports that every person on his staff adjusted quickly to coming to the office early. "If he's got a real problem, he'll get up in time to be at the office to get the help he needs," relates this broker. "It's to everyone's advantage that problems are solved as quickly as possible without having to wait until the day of a regular sales meeting. It's to management's advantage that individual problems do not take up the time of the entire selling staff. Whenever a situation develops which we feel the whole staff should know about and understand, we put it on the sales meeting agenda."

Avoid asking people to attend a meeting that has no value to them personally or professionally. They'll resent wasting their time and as a result it will take them at least twice as long to gear into the day's work. This form of resentment is called "mental down time" and it can affect the whole staff. Those whose time was wasted will be articulate martyrs and those who have to listen to them will be too embarrassed to admit they got something from the meeting.

Whether in formal sales meetings, one-to-one conferences or a "salesperson's hour," the important point to remember is that there's a continuing need to communicate in both directions and an endless variety of ways to do it. How well management succeeds will depend on how well they prepare in advance.

1. Sherwin, "Management *of* Objectives," *Harvard Business Review,* May/ June 1976.
2. Clark, *Brainstorming,* p. 71.
3. Osborn, *Applied Imagination,* p. 156.

CHAPTER 3

Preparation

When a meeting runs smoothly is it because someone planned it that way? When a meeting achieves its objective for both salespeople and management it is largely because those responsible spent time in preparation. Starting with an objective, then developing materials and an agenda that support it is the surest road to a successful sales meeting.

Top management people in real estate firms with a good track record in both sales meetings and *sales* stress over and over again the importance of spending time preparing for every meeting. They say it is some of their most productive time, whether they are selling brokers in small firms or full time management people in multi-office corporations. Each does the job in his own way but they all follow certain principles.

START WITH AN IDEA BANK

Start by having one place where everything that relates to sales meetings is collected—a bank of ideas and reminders. The bank is perhaps a drawer in your desk, part of a file drawer or a notebook where everything is written down as it comes to mind. The important thing is having one place where everything can be put and forming the habit of putting everything in that one place. Then when the time comes to prepare for a meeting there's not a scramble to locate ideas, notes and other reminders. In the words of one REALTOR®, "a short pencil is better than a long memory."

Here are a few of the things sales managers collect in their idea banks.

> Reminders: Names of salespeople who should be complimented and why. Follow-up items from previous meetings.
> Training techniques that need to be introduced or reviewed.
> Ideas: For selling, listing, financing, advertising, promotion.
> News: Finance, local industry, regulations, people.
> Professional development: Books, magazine articles, lectures, courses, meetings.
> Sources: Films, tapes, speakers, books, magazines, pamphlets.
> Fun and games: Cartoons, contests, promotions, games.

Some brokers carry a few 3 x 5" cards around with them and jot down ideas as they come. Then at the end of the day they drop the cards into the idea bank along with collected news clippings, tear sheets from magazines, book reviews, ads, letters —the reminders they'll need in whatever form they come to their attention.

The idea bank is a good repository for reminders of the extras that are important to the meeting participants. Such ideas include the names of people to be praised for getting a difficult listing or completing a problem sale, mention of recognition they've got in the press for professional or civic achievements; details of awards to be made at the meeting, whether they involve a contest in progress or the regular presentation of commission checks or a fresh flower to brighten the desks of salespeople who have closed a sale within the week.

Fun and games items suggest ways to liven a meeting with a quick game, perhaps something to use between opening announcements and information exchange and the longer time spent on the meeting's objective.

In addition to supplying all these meeting ideas, the bank has another benefit. As you become more attuned to watch for things to use in meetings you also become better informed in general. As you search for successful sales techniques whether in the field of psychology, communications, time management or product knowledge you become more knowledgeable about what is going on all around you. The inevitable result is that you develop a sense of how what is going on in the rest of the world relates to the world of real estate and pass it along to the others in the firm.

A MEETING HAS TO SATISFY MANY PEOPLE

Meeting materials and methods have to satisfy the needs of a variety of people. Whatever the objective for a meeting or a series of them, a degree of flexibility in how it will be presented is important. What seems to be the best or perhaps the only way to treat a topic may turn off the people who have to go out and put it into practice. Look for several approaches or solutions to problems. A wholly new use of old techniques and systems can pay real dividends when it sends the sales staff out to give it a try.

A flexible manager maintains a certain detachment from routines and the fixed customs of the business. He can even manage to have a reasonable detachment from his own past attitudes and habits of mind, dismissing long-held pet theories of what will work and what won't.

Many management people today who fret about the limitations being imposed on our basic freedoms from outside sources may be overlooking the self-imposed limitations of their own fixed ideas and habits. A search for exciting new ways to present knowledge, develop skills and influence the attitudes of sales-people also serves to generate self-renewal in management.

EACH WEEK BRINGS A NEW SITUATION

Every sales meeting must respond to a new situation. It doesn't matter whether the firm has had the same salespeople for years; every time they meet both the people and their needs are different than the last time they got together. Their personal needs (remember Maslow's hierarchy of needs) have altered at least a little bit and their selling situations are never the same from one week to the next. Last week's big problem has either been solved or has grown bigger while this week brought new challenges and opportunities. Management's needs have changed, too. The firm is either closer to its goals, just where it was a week ago or it has fallen behind.

What goes into the preparation for a sales meeting will be influenced by the situation that exists at the moment for both the firm and the salespeople. A manager who stays on top of these factors and learns to deal with them week by week is the one who comes up with a realistic objective and the know-how to help the staff to find their own solutions and fill their own needs so the whole group "makes it."

GETTING STARTED

Learn how much material can be used in a single meeting. In addition to the main objective, time is needed to cover weekly essentials. Allotted time disappears fast even during early planning stages. An agenda outline is helpful in keeping a good balance between the most important things to be accomplished and all the extras that seem to merit some of that valuable time.

Assuming the main objective is already set, the next step is to list the essentials that are part of every week's meeting, the things that cannot be handled in any other way. (Or could they? Perhaps this is where to be creative in another way.) Regular items in many meetings include a brief of new listings, problems or changes in older listings and the needs of individual salespeople for certain kinds of properties. A sharing of successes of the past week allows management a chance to praise those who've done well and, it is hoped, inspire the rest to earn praise next time around. All this takes time—a minimum of one minute per salesperson, maybe 15 or 20 minutes altogether. The time and items are written on your working agenda.

Next, a brief change of pace? Meetings that have an ebb and flow of serious-light-serious help keep the participants alert. At this point in the agenda two minutes of fun in the form of a quickie game or funny stories may be desirable. (But don't let the meeting bog down here and become a story-telling session. Remember that earlier complaint: *The meeting gets off the track and time is wasted in unrelated chit-chat.*) Think of a way to use the game or funny story to lead into the next, serious part of the meeting. Thus far, 22 minutes' meeting time is allotted.

Now, take the objective and develop an outline of what materials/techniques will be used to achieve it and what salespeople will be told they'll learn if they participate.

WORKING ON THE MAIN OBJECTIVE

Write out the objective. It will be needed later for the meeting anyway. Once it is in writing, you can, in a sense, step back and look at it, examining ways to present it as a challenge to the sales staff.

For example, let's say the objective is *how we can get more listings.*

EXAMINE THE PROBLEM THOROUGHLY
First, the facts

Listings are down.
The market is flooded with FSBO signs and ads.

Listings are going to competitors.

Listings are expiring and not being renewed.

The firm has a number of new, inexperienced salespeople.

Next, questions about the market area

Is the market so hot that owners believe they can sell properties themselves?

Are the listings being lost the kind of properties the firm wants?

Is the money market so tight properties that could be sold cannot be financed?

Then, management questions

How well has the firm been servicing its listings? Do we have records to prove it?

Which salesperson has been doing the best job?

Is there a routine set up for salespeople to follow?

Has management kept check on salespeople's performance?

How aggressively has new business been pursued?

Has management reviewed listing techniques lately?

Has the staff been asked to discuss listing problems in a sales meeting?

How much time are salespeople spending to cultivate new contacts?

What are they doing along this line?

Finally, management analyzes management

Does the firm know what its share of the market should be?

How does the firm rate with others in getting listings?

What has been done by other REALTORS® that this firm hasn't tried?

What sources of finance haven't been tapped?

Has a guaranteed sales plan been explored?

DEVELOPING THE PROGRAM

After completing this examination of facts, you are ready to develop a program or perhaps a whole series of programs that will challenge salespeople to come up with good, practical ways to get more listings. Your challenge is to make the meetings so *new* that the sales staff will go out from the meetings motivated to put their added knowledge and sharpened skills to work immediately.

Three techniques suggest themselves for this meeting: discussion, brainstorming and role play. With these three or perhaps in conjunction with them, consider the use of audio/visuals.

Discussion

Make it new by having the salespeople discuss the challenge. Give them a couple lead questions that generate a positive approach to the objective so they do not bog down in discussing everything that's being done wrong, with questions like "What could we be doing differently that would bring us new listings?" or "What are some of the ways we could be servicing our present listings better?"

Prepare for such a discussion by making notes of the points to be covered and questions they should center on. Once again, a short pencil is better than a long memory. What is written down is there to remind you as the meeting speeds along. That way there is no chance of the main point of a discussion being overlooked.

Brainstorming

Make it new by encouraging all the new salespeople to suggest their ideas. (Remember the complaint: *If you're new to real estate, your speculations and suggestions are not valued. And quite often you're not encouraged to contribute them.*) New people bring a pair of fresh eyes to the business and aren't fettered by the chains of tradition. Many things they suggest may not work but if one of them comes up with one workable idea it might be worth thousands to the staff and the firm. And that one person having been recognized will encourage the rest to keep thinking up fresh, new ideas to contribute.

Role play

Make it new by asking two inexperienced or less successful salespeople to assume the "Mr. and Mrs. For Sale by Owner" roles, to be interviewed by the best lister on the staff. What they learn from him won't cost them a penny more than their time in the meeting and it could result in getting many listings they might otherwise lose.

Most REALTORS® wouldn't dream of sending new salespeople out on a FSBO call until they acquire some experience. Where could they get better experience in using their training than by role play with someone who knows the answers *and* most of the questions and is skilled in handling this difficult situation? Experienced salespeople benefit, too, by being reminded of techniques they may have been overlooking.

The foregoing example suggests just a few techniques and approaches management can adapt to challenge any staff to solve a wide variety of problems. An almost infinite list of suggestions and sources is given in the chapter on meeting topics; valuable reading and study materials are listed in the bibliography; further text on how management can develop good communications with staff can be found in the chapter on group communication techniques.

Now choose an approach to the objective, decide what materials can be used or what meeting form will fit into the time allotted. Having already assigned about 22 minutes' time, there remain perhaps 30 to 35 minutes for the major part of the one hour meeting. A few minutes will be needed to summarize what has been accomplished toward achieving the stated objective.

If you decide to use the last minute or two to ask the staff for final participation, ask for some one-liners on what can be done in the week ahead or what the individual salespeople like most about the company they are affiliated with or what each person can do to improve the company's position in the market or its image in the community.

Audio/visuals

If none of the three techniques suggested earlier seems a good way to help achieve a meeting's objective, you may decide to use audio/visuals. When audio/visuals of any kind are programmed, a dry run in advance is important. First, this will show whether the concepts the material presents are in line with your policy and provide the information and help you want. Second, it also will show whether it relates to the meeting objective.

Films and cassettes

Advance preparation in the use of either films or cassette tapes includes marking places where the machine will be stopped to allow discussion of a point just covered and to explore with the staff how to use it in their daily work. The dual benefit here is not only the discussion, but the need of the audience for a series of "participation breaks" that prevent boredom, drowsiness and the resulting loss of attention.

Whatever you do, don't run through a whole film or cassette without a break. A generally accepted rule of thumb is that you should break a film or cassette session every ten minutes or so. Less than ten-minute breaks tend to destroy the message. Letting it run much longer than ten risks losing the audience's attention.

What should you do at a break? You could choose a place where a problem has been presented or a situation set up. Then *before* the solution is given, stop the film or tape and get your people involved in that problem. You might set up a quick, spontaneous role play, assigning roles and asking the people how the situation is likely to evolve and how they would want it to be resolved. A question and answer session is another way to handle it but be prepared with good, logical questions. Maybe the problem situation could have been avoided with different handling of it in advance of the dilemma. Ask for ideas along this line. As you grow more accustomed to doing this sort of thing with films and cassettes you'll find how they can add zip and introduce outside talent into your meetings. You get tired of doing it all yourself. Your staff needs the variety, too.

Overhead projectors

Overhead projectors are popular presentation tools because they most effectively control the participation of an audience. The viewers are seeing what you are saying, which allows little or no opportunity for their minds to wander. The retention factor of material presented in this way is said to be eight times more effective than through straight oral presentation. (To use an overhead projector, you place a transparency on the stage [base] after turning on the machine and focusing a lens head. The image reflects through an apparatus at the top of the assembly onto a screen. You can use either prepared film or write with a grease pencil on a clear 8 x 10" film while you talk.)

If an overhead projector will be used, rehearse the material carefully. It's good to have somebody else work with you at least part of the rehearsal time. This second person can check two things: The visibility of the projection, whether it can be seen from any point in the room and whether your position is interfering with visibility; and the legibility of what is being printed or written. Figures that are too small result in failure to make an important point. An audience will strain to see illegible material only so long, then give up in despair.

One important caveat in using any film equipment: Always be sure there's a spare bulb on hand! Bulbs have a way of burning out at the most inopportune moment. If there's a spare one close at hand, the changeover can be made with a minimum of interruption. If not, the whole meeting goes up for grabs.

Whatever materials or meeting form is to be used, the manager who develops a working agenda as he goes along is bound to come up to meeting time better prepared than if he has to extemporize. The sample agenda presented here suggests some of the things to cover in such a working paper. Do it in such a way that it serves company and staff needs. A couple of points ought to be emphasized.

SAMPLE WORKING AGENDA

Meeting date   January 3   Start at 8:30 a.m.   End at 9:30 a.m.

Time	Agenda	Notes
8:30	Meeting objective: HOW WE CAN GET MORE LISTINGS	
8:31	Staff reports: Listings, sales	State just the facts—1 minute maximum—everybody listen, no side talk—saves time
8:45	Commission checks, other recognition	JB new Rotary president AB elected library board
	Special problems: listing prices, new properties wanted	Whole staff
9:00	Stand and stretch—quickie game or joke	Manager
9:02	Restate objective and what this meeting should accomplish: HOW WE CAN GET MORE LISTINGS by using new techniques and broader acquaintance in the market. *Goal: Ten new ideas*	
	Appoint a meeting recorder	Susie B
	Discussion: Facts about firm's market share	Manager
	New techniques 　What works and how to try it 　Are we doing all we can to service our present listings?	Harry B's new idea plus rest of staff
	How to develop new contacts in the area	Mary M's suggestion
	How many new contacts in last month?	
9:25	Susie B reads list of new ideas	
	Summarize—what we can do this week	Manager
9:28	"Pluses" from any team member—one liners	
9:30	Adjourn	

This sample agenda illustrates one way to organize the topical content, time allotments and notations to remind you who is to participate and when. Make your agenda fit your own style of meeting. Agendas also serve as a place to record follow-up notes as the meeting progresses. Used in this fashion, they become a permanent record of what you planned, what took place and what you need to do as follow-up.

Keeping track of available time is important from the very beginning. It will help in eliminating non-essentials from the meeting plan and it will aid in keeping the meeting on track as it proceeds. It will provide advance reminders of everything needed for the meeting, what should be checked out ahead of time and which people to check with to be sure they're ready to participate. It will also help spot places where the people who don't usually participate can be encouraged to take a more active part.

If agendas are kept from past meetings they help a sales manager review what's been done over a period of time, avoiding the monotony of repeating the same routines and maybe even the same subject matter week after week.

EXTRAS ON THE AGENDA

(Complaint: *There's never a chance to introduce something we want to talk about.*)

If not every week, then at least once a month, the agenda should provide some time for staff to introduce things they have on their minds. Three or four minutes ought to be enough time as a starter. Then, if the subject deserves more time or needs interim research or investigation, you can defer it to a future meeting. This does not imply that it's simply put off in the hopes it will be forgotten, but rather that after further discussion and work by management and/or staff it will be on the agenda at a stated future time.

WHAT *NOT* TO PUT ON THE AGENDA

Adverse criticism of any kind, directed at individuals, belongs in a one-to-one conference with the person at fault. Matters of this kind should never be part of a sales meeting.

Other problems of a more general nature that involve only one staff member or a few at most also ought to be handled separately. If, as a result of these individual conferences, a new company policy evolves or if some new ways to correct a bad situation are developed, then they may have a place in a sales meeting.

Even problems of a general nature should not always be dealt with in a sales meeting. For example, poor attendance or tardiness may be a major concern to a sales manager. But when he talks about it in a sales meeting, chances are better than equal that those he needs to reach aren't present! Why should people who show up on time suffer a manager's sermonizing about those who don't? After all, everyone there came to be helped and encouraged, not to be criticized.

Don't put unrelated "fillers" on an agenda. When you don't have enough material for a full meeting, cut down the meeting length. Some broker/managers say they have occasional meetings that last only 10 to 15 minutes. This usually happens when things are running smoothly and the salespeople are so busy they're better off getting out on the street to take care of business.

FINAL CHECK ON LOGISTICS

Once the meeting agenda is firmed up it should be checked for logistics.

Will the meeting room be arranged to suit the kind of session planned?

Will the necessary equipment be available and in good running order?

Who will be responsible for seeing that paper, pencils, chalk and other supplies are in the room before the meeting starts?

If food is to be served who will be responsible for clearing it away before the meeting starts?

If refreshments are to be served during meeting breaks who will be responsible for it?

HOW TO ANNOUNCE THE MEETING

Meeting announcements, like meeting content, reflect the individual style of the firm and its management. Some companies issue announcements to each salesperson, meeting by meeting. Others provide a monthly schedule of sales meetings and all the other company events they hope salespeople will attend. Still others never provide printed announcements, expecting the sales staff to know the meeting is going to be held every week at the same time in the same place. When the routine is altered, one notice is posted on the office bulletin board.

Limitations of either time or budget or both needn't restrict creativity in meeting announcements.

There are times when a straightforward, typed agenda announcement of an important company conference is best. Such announcements give more details of what is planned for a half- or whole-day session, perhaps including names of the participants in the program. The formality of such an announcement has a lot to recommend it.

At other times, the idea bank will provide the special touch needed to attract the staff's attention and attendance.

A cartoon, clipped from a newspaper or magazine, which emphasizes in a funny way the unrelenting work needed to make a sale or get one's foot in the door or keep that same foot out of one's mouth can be photocopied for use on a meeting announcement. Everybody encounters difficult situations and people and when it can be pointed up in an announcement as a human condition rather than a sticky situation limited to real estate, salespeople are likely to read it at once. When this happens, the idea bank has paid off.

Or a news headline, clipped from the local newspaper, announcing an industry or plant moving into the local market, could alert the staff that the meeting will deal with the new listings that will be needed to supply housing for the new people. Or it could focus on some phase of relocation selling that management wants to discuss and exert special effort on in the immediate or long-range future. That same headline could announce a meeting dealing with the need for broader acquaintance in the general business community. Another idea bank payoff.

Business stationers usually stock 8½ x 11" letterheads imprinted with artwork suitable for meeting announcements. Some of them even have preprinted headings for different types of meetings or that are related to seasonal events. Most of the page is left vacant for messages to be typed or hand-lettered in.

Photocopy machines offer almost unlimited possibilities for creating the firm's own custom-tailored meeting announcements. These might combine reproduction of a new promotion piece, a hand-lettered announcement of time and place and perhaps a typed two or three liner on the meeting's objective.

WHAT TO INCLUDE IN THE ANNOUNCEMENT

There are wide differences of opinion among real estate management people about whether meeting announcements should contain specific details of what is being planned for the meeting.

Those who give details believe people come better prepared to contribute their ideas and experiences. In this group, a number of sales managers report that their meeting notices include "suggested" reading for meeting preparation by salespeople. It could be an article in *real estate today*®, a feature from the state association bulletin or a state Chamber of Commerce publication, a chapter from the *Real Estate Sales Handbook* or some other book in the company library. Some firms say their people take the cue and do preliminary reading on their own. Those who simply announce the topic believe that's all their people want or need to know in advance.

Many firms haven't decided which method they prefer, so they use one method part of the time, the other the rest of the time.

The following pages illustrate a variety of sales meeting notices that range from a single office to the large annual meeting of a multi-office firm with more than 300 sales associates.

A B C, REALTORS®

RESIDENTIAL SALES MEETING AGENDA FOR NOVEMBER 19__
— MAIN STREET HOLIDAY INN —

    I. Invocation and Pledge of Allegiance
   II. New Sales Associates Presentation—Dick Heinz
  III. NATIONAL ASSOCIATION OF REALTORS®' Convention Review
      A. Don Erskine
      B. Lucille Dean
      C. John Cramer
  IV. Customer Relations Program
      A. Joe Rowan
      B. Chuck Denver
      C. Louise West
   V. Inter-office Referral Game—Dick Heinz
  VI. A B C, REALTORS®—A house-sold Word
      "Delivering a successful listing presentation and techniques of closing the Seller."—Moderator, Tom Reed
      A. Ted Vernon
      B. Paul Johnson
      C. Steve Boone
 VII. Top Sales and Listing Awards (Silver Trays)—Dick Heinz
VIII. Top Sales and Listing Awards (Gifts)—Dick Heinz
  IX. Referral Checks Presentation—John Cramer
   X. Bonus Checks Presentation—Dick Heinz
  XI. Adjourn

ABC, REALTORS®

TO: All Personnel
           West, Far West and Northwest

FROM: Art Carney, President

SUBJECT: June Sales Meeting Dates
           June 1 —Individual Office Meeting
           June 8 —Individual Office Meeting
           June 10—Sales Managers Seminar
                   9 a.m.–5 p.m.
                   Lower Level Meeting Room
                   Main St. Office
           June 11—General Sales Meeting
                   8:30 a.m.—Forum Community House
                   Antreville
           June 15—Individual Office Meeting
           June 22—Individual Office Meeting
           June 30—Quarterly Staff Sales Seminar
                   9 a.m.—Lower Level Meeting Room
                   Main St. Office

ALL
SALES
ASSOCIATES

LET'S GET AWAY FROM IT ALL!

WHY: SALES MEETING

WHERE: GLEN ELLYN HOLIDAY INN

WHEN: WEDNESDAY, FEB. 18th
   8:00 A.M. COFFEE & ROLLS
   8:30 A.M. MEETING

YOU ARE ALL INVITED!
PLEASE COME !!!

Dick Stern

2-16-76

General Sales
- Meeting -
Wed., November 19th
at the
Pikes Peak Hilton
Longmont Rd, Colorado Springs

DON'T MISS A DYNAMIC PRESENTATION ON. . .

* Delivering a successful listing presentation

* Creative techniques of closing the seller

* Consumerism today -- customer relations program

* The NATIONAL ASSOCIATION OF REALTORS®
  Convention review

Coffee + Rolls
8:00 A.M.

Meeting
8:30 A.M.

CHAPTER 4

Logistics

LOGISTICS DEFINED

Logistics, best known as the military science that deals with procurement, movement and maintenance of facilities and personnel, are just as important to the science of successful sales meetings.

What are the elements of sales meeting logistics? They are the location and the physical arrangement of the meeting room, the timing of the meetings, plus the equipment needed to get the message across.

The physical arrangements and setting of sales meetings contribute greatly to their success. Environment of a meeting room is important to both good attendance and attention.

As you read this chapter, bear in mind that it presents *ideal* standards. Very few real estate firms are in a position to invest in all the facilities or equipment suggested. But you can glean ideas here that are practical for your operation and within the limits of your budget by taking the ideal, adding your own creativity and improving and changing whatever you're not satisfied with.

Here are some comments of REALTORS® regarding meeting logistics.

> "We get them together in the morning, while they're fresh."
> "We get them away from their desks because desk tops are distracting."
> "We keep them free of telephone and people distractions."
> "We change the location occasionally."
> "We meet at the same time every week."
> "We schedule 'field trips' now and then."
> "We feed them." (Usually breakfast.)
> "We give them coffee and donuts or sweet rolls but clear all food away before starting a meeting."
> "We make them comfortable but not *too* comfortable."
> "We vary the seating arrangement to suit the meeting."

The list could go on. These are the points made most frequently in firms known for their fine sales meetings.

PRIVACY IS IMPORTANT

It's best if meetings are held where the group is insulated from the distractions of ringing telephones or people coming in or passing by. If sales meetings must be held in the office, try to schedule them before or after regular business hours.

Assign one person to answer the phone and take messages. This routine need not involve any falsehoods. A direct statement to the effect that the person is not available but will return the call by a specified time will almost always satisfy the caller.

Interruptions by visitors are harder to handle when meetings are held in the office. Passersby can see the staff (unless they're in a closed meeting or conference room) and most of the time outsiders feel no reluctance about coming in. One problem of the real estate business is that salespeople are expected to be at the beck and call of sellers and buyers 24 hours a day. The growing trend of professionalism may gradually change this. It will take a lot of training on the part of salespeople to educate the public that certain hours are off limits. Put in the context that sales meetings are just as important to sellers and buyers as they are to salespeople, the job may be easier to do. Those sales meetings are where salespeople exchange information on properties available and wanted—very important topics to the people they serve. After all, salespeople are not available to callers when they are out working with buyers or sellers, so it ought to be a matter of course that there are other times when business takes them away from the phone and the office.

THE PHYSICAL SETTING

Salespeople are taught how to arrange the most favorable setting possible when they are working to obtain a listing, qualify a buyer or negotiate the sale of a property. With this kind of training, it is natural that they should expect the same favorable setting when management is trying to sell (translate "teach") them new skills, impart knowledge or influence their attitude toward their work.

Whatever is done to make sure the meeting place is the best the firm can provide and is arranged to accommodate both the sales manager and the sales staff in the best possible way is time and money well spent. This investment is good because it can help translate meeting objectives into desired action.

GET THEM AWAY FROM THEIR DESKS

Get the salespeople away from their desks if at all possible. There are a number of reasons why this is important. It's impossible to hold the attention of a salesperson who sits looking at a desk top filled with reminders of things waiting to be done. Ringing telephones are an almost certain interruption even when the office secretary or someone else is assigned to answer them and take messages.

What do you do when there's absolutely no chance of meeting at another location? One imaginative broker, forced to work within these restrictions, has his salespeople turn their chairs around and face *away* from their desks. He reports this not only takes their attention away from papers on their desks but that it prods everyone to clear desk tops at least for the duration of the meeting since somebody else will be looking at it.

In this particular broker's case, the chair turnaround also results in the sales manager being the only one in the room who faces the front door and street traffic, which cuts down on distractions and discourages passersby from dropping in.

WHAT IS THE IDEAL MEETING ROOM?

For the firms that have one, a conference room provides the best possible setting for most sales meetings. Closed off from the rest of the office, away from street distractions and ringing telephones, the meetings are easier to control.

Proximity to office records is another plus. Even the most carefully prepared meeting will occasionally need records and other materials from office files. When sales meetings are held in-house these supplemental materials can be gotten quickly;

otherwise, discussions based on them must be postponed to a later meeting and the opportunities for immediate action are lost.

Finally, when meetings are held in-house, little time is lost by the staff in moving from the meeting room to their desks. The "9:05 rule" is operative here: actions instituted in the meeting are activated within five minutes of the meeting's close.

DO YOU HAVE EQUIPMENT AND FACILITIES TO USE IT?

In a day when there is a growing use of audio/visual materials in sales meetings and training sessions it is important to use them in suitable surroundings.

Films shown in a less-than-darkened room lose much if not most of their effectiveness. Overhead projectors need less space than films or film strips but they also need a darkened room. Cassettes and tapes require a room that can be soundproofed against the intrusion of outside noises.

If the company office lacks either the equipment or suitable meeting room to use it, look for other meeting places that are equipped and available at little or no added cost.

LIGHTING

Get enough light in the room so both the speaker and his materials can be seen clearly. When an audience can't see, they'll strain for a while, then give up in disgust. After all, why should they think it's important if the person using it hasn't bothered to make it easy to see?

If the speaker is talking at a podium, be sure it's well lighted so he can read text or refer to notes comfortably. Be sure the speaker isn't facing directly into a spotlight or the glare of outside light that cuts out the faces of his listeners.

If the salespeople are expected to read or write at their chairs, the lighting over that area of the room should be good, too.

AIR

If the same meeting room is used frequently and is not air-conditioned, it may be possible to install exhaust fans that change the air at regular intervals. Rotating electric fans can help keep the air moving but be sure to place them where they don't blow on the group. Put them along the walls or well behind the speaker. Somebody is sure to get up and turn off a fan that's near him, because the whirring noise prevents his hearing what's being said. If the fan is placed well behind the speaker and he can hear it, he will speak loudly enough to be heard.

Cigarette, cigar and pipe smoke are meeting room problems. A growing number of non-smokers express resentment at having to endure other people's smoke. If a room can be divided in such a way that non-smokers are separated from smokers so the smoke doesn't blow in their direction, everybody will be happier and in a more receptive mood.

SOUND

Ideally, the meeting room should shut out every intruding sound from the outside. If the company conference room is used and Muzak or other electronic sound is piped into the offices, shut it off. Other intrusive sounds—ringing telephones, street noises and office conversation—have been discussed elsewhere. Everything possible should be done to shut these out of the meeting. When meetings are held in public buildings such as motels and hotels, precautions should be taken to prevent sound intrusions from adjoining rooms. Folding screen walls do not shut out sounds from adjoining spaces, so be sure competing meetings will not be held in the area next to the one your firm has reserved.

Sound facilities inside the room should be the best affordable. When meetings are small there's no need for amplifying equipment. As the size of the meeting increases, however, be sure every word spoken to the group can be heard.

Fuzzy amplification equipment ought not be used if you care whether the audience hears what's being said. It's like going to see a film in a cut-rate theater where the price is low because the sound equipment is inferior. One gets the picture but not the message!

The motors of sound projectors, used for reel or slide films, have a distracting noise when set down in the middle of the group in large meetings. Try to place the projector as far back as possible.

MEETING AWAY FROM THE OFFICE

A growing number of REALTORS® hold sales meetings away from the office. Many believe a combination breakfast-and-sales meeting works best because it brings the group together early in the day, starts on a pleasant social note of a meal together and is in a private setting, removed from office distractions. Those who use private dining rooms in restaurants, hotels or motels say they accomplish more in less time and that their salespeople like the change of scene for the same reasons.

Meetings like this, of course, cost more. But weighted in a true cost/effectiveness ratio they might prove to be less expensive and more productive than those held in an unsatisfactory office setting.

Other locations work well for certain kinds of meetings although they are not usually available on a regular basis. These include meeting rooms at

Savings and loan institutions
Banks
Public libraries
Universities
Schools
Churches
Hospitals
Public recreation halls

Some of these institutions have audio/visual equipment they are willing to let others use on the premises, even on occasion providing someone to operate the equipment. Tax-supported institutions sometimes allow taxpayers to use meeting rooms at no charge. It pays to know what facilities exist in the area and who should be contacted if the firm wants to use them. Such records can be kept in the "idea bank" discussed earlier.

MEETING ROOM SETUPS

There is nothing standard about room setups. Every meeting has different requirements in almost infinite combinations. The kinds of chairs used, whether they should be arranged theater-style, placed at desks or conference tables or moved about as the meeting progresses will depend on the kind of meeting being planned. The one constant is the need to be flexible and creative because you usually have limited furnishings and equipment.

Ask any homemaker why she changes the furniture around occasionally. The answer is likely to be, "I got tired of it the way it was. It was time for a change."

One sales manager/broker reports that when he wants to introduce a new sales approach or wants to brainstorm new ideas for old problems he starts by rearranging the meeting room. When his sales staff comes into a rearranged meeting room they know the meeting topic will involve change.

The meeting objective and materials to be presented have a bearing on the room arrangement. A theater-type arrangement is fine for a telling session; a flexible seating arrangement is needed when part of the meeting is devoted to telling and another segment to small buzz groups or role playing. Many small meetings are best set up at round or rectangular tables where the group can work face to face.

AVOID "BLIND" PLACES

Chairs and writing facilities for weekly sales meetings of up to ten people can be a conference table "T" arrangement where you sit at the head and others sit opposite each other at the sides and far end. You can look directly at each person and they can see you clearly. But if people are seated at your left or right, they are in "blind" places where they cannot see you and you cannot see them and watch their reactions.

CHAIRS

Seating ought to be comfortable but not too comfortable. Uncomfortable seating results in a squirming audience that finds it hard to concentrate on what's being said or done. Chairs that are too comfortable lull people into a state of ease that reduces their attention span drastically.

Some firms with special training facilities use chairs with a side arm writing surface. Such equipment is easy to move about as the meeting needs change from a listening/lecture segment to buzz sessions or small discussion or role playing groups.

DESKS

Many real estate firms must find ways to conduct sales meetings within the confines of a bull-pen arrangement of the main office space. As stated earlier, if this is the only space available, try to have desk tops cleared or have the staff turn their chairs around to face the desk in back of them. This at least removes the distraction of their own papers and records. But unless that desk has a cleared top, the other person's paper work may prove to be an interesting distraction to the person facing it, even testing his ability to read upside down!

CONFERENCE TABLES

If a conference room is available it is usually equipped with a table salespeople can use as a writing surface during the meeting. Standard size rectangular conference tables seat ten comfortably but have limited space for papers, notebooks and the like. Round tables that accommodate eight are good for discussion meetings where participants should sit facing each other.

The meeting leader of a small group, seated at one end of a conference table, is in close proximity to those he is working with and in clear view of all of them. It is a more authoritative position than a round table offers. On the other hand, a round table has the advantage of no "authority position," thereby enhancing open exchange of ideas and opinions.

TEACHING EQUIPMENT

Useful equipment for modern sales meetings ranges from a traditional chalkboard or a pad of poster size newsprint paper set on a tripod easel to sophisticated electronic audio/visual devices for showing films, film strips, slides, overhead projectors, cassette tapes and audio or video tape for instant playback of role plays. A big budget for equipment is fine but it is not essential to having successful meetings. The creativity of an imaginative sales manager can produce exciting results through clever use of simple teaching tools.

Some of the most productive brainstorming sessions are recorded on easel paper with a grease pencil, like the brainstorm session reported by one successful, large firm that uses this simple device to record their salespeople's ideas on new approaches to For Sale By Owner situations. The sales manager understands his people and knows they'll implement their own ideas faster than they will his. He writes their ideas as fast as he can, paying no attention to whether or not he finds their ideas acceptable.

When he wants to encourage participation by someone who has not contributed an idea, he stops and addresses that person: "Martha, out of all these ideas, which one could you add onto?" The broker who uses this technique happens to have more than 300 sales associates. A firm with less than ten could use it just as effectively.

In a large meeting room, perhaps the kind used for a general sales meeting in a large firm, this same brainstorming information might be more dramatically presented and easier for all to read if it were written on an overhead projector film. The projection screen should be placed high enough for all to see and well above the person doing the writing.

ROOM ARRANGEMENTS

Edward J. Hegarty, former director of sales training with a division of Westinghouse, whose experience in staging meetings covers more than 40 years, says chairs should be set up so that the entrance to the meeting is at the rear. Then anyone coming into the room can be seen by the speaker but not by the audience. If the entrance is behind the speaker, the audience sees those who go by or come in.

Salespeople's backs should be to the windows. Don't let them blink at that outdoor light. Besides, they might watch the window washer across the street or traffic on the avenue, and sales managers are not selling window washing or street traffic!

When chairs are faced away from the window, the light should help show props or charts and it will help listeners see better.

For large meetings try to have the speaker above the level of the seating unless a center aisle is open for the speaker to move into the group. If he stays in a static position on the same level as the audience, some of them can't see him or his visual aids. When they can't see, they lose interest.

If slide or reel films are to be shown with the speaker at the front of the room, the lectern should be at right so the speaker looks over his right shoulder toward the screen. It's not only more comfortable for him but permits him to use a hand or electric pointer with ease. Of course, for a left-handed speaker the reverse arrangement is best.

The following drawings show three popular arrangements for meeting rooms. A fourth, the theater seating arrangement, is so simple it does not require a drawing. It consists of row on row of chairs facing a podium or stage with either a center aisle or side aisles, depending on the size of the room and whether or not films will be shown. If films are to be used there should be an open aisle or clear space from the projection equipment to the screen so the people seated in the audience are not silhouetted against the screen.

These are principles of ideal room arrangement. Don't be put off by the area shown; adapt your equipment to your own space.

THE LEADER OR SPEAKER IS UP FRONT, ALONE

Whether the meeting is a small group at a conference table or several hundred people assembled for a general sales meeting, give the speaker the spotlight, alone. At a small conference table he can sit at one end; at a round table he sits in the group. If there is a platform, have it used by one person at a time, never occupied by anyone other than the person speaking, regardless of rank in the company. This rule is violated over and over again. When other people are up front with the speaker they are drawing the teeth of his message even if they never move an eyelash, which isn't likely!

Whenever one of these freeloaders clears his throat, lights a cigarette, looks at his watch, crosses his legs, makes a note or—horror of horrors—dozes off, he draws attention of the audience away from the speaker who at that very moment may be making his most salient and telling point. If the speaker is good enough to be up there speaking to the group, he deserves their undivided attention.

The exception to this rule is a panel discussion. There, a moderator may be at center table or on his feet at the side,

Single conference table setup

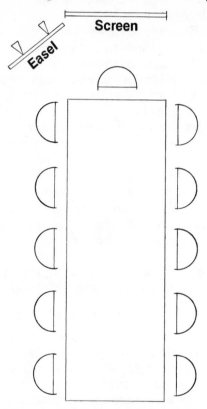

With the single conference table setup, a small group is accommodated, while still giving the leader a position of authority. This arrangement is popular for small discussion groups and informal "telling" sessions, yet it can easily adapt into a more formalized meeting where reports are given.

Conference setup

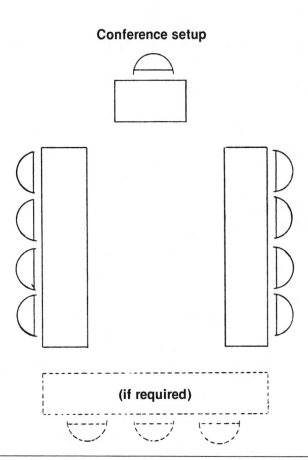

In a regular conference setup, the leader is in a position of authority with full visibility to and from him to everyone in the group, even in a large group where many tables are needed. Only one side of each table should have chairs, as illustrated.

Lecture-in-the-round for demonstrations to small groups

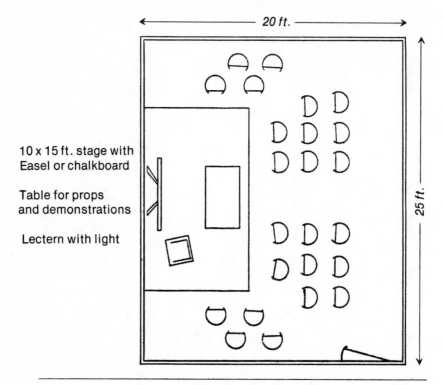

10 x 15 ft. stage with
Easel or chalkboard

Table for props
and demonstrations

Lectern with light

A lecture-in-the-round arrangement is adaptable for a variety of meetings. The open center aisle allows the speaker to move into the audience, a great help in generating full audience participation. Up front, the lectern and easel are ideal equipment for most small groups. A portable screen could be added here for film use. A flat surface table would be needed for overhead projector materials.

acting as the catalyst between the audience and however many panelists are involved.

FOOD

REALTORS® have divided opinions on whether or not it is good to serve food or to meet regularly during or after a meal. Some bring sweet rolls or donuts to the office the morning of the weekly meeting and serve them with coffee. Some continue serving food and beverages through the meeting; others have a cut-off time, usually the announced time for the meeting to begin, and remove all plates, cups, etc. before the meeting. Latecomers miss the treat.

Firms that invite their people to breakfast in a restaurant, motel or hotel say they meet early for the meal, have the tables cleared and start the meeting at 8:00 or 8:30 so the staff can be back at the office and start the day's work on schedule.

Luncheon and dinner meetings are usually restricted to general sales conferences, held monthly, quarterly or annually. At these events the meal may be the break in an all-day session or a special function or celebration culminating a series of sales meetings or a year's efforts. As such, they are not really a part of the regular sales meeting program but are considered special events.

CHOOSING THE DAY OF THE WEEK

Activity in the local market influences the choice of day of the week sales meetings are held. It seems most brokers have their regular meetings early in the week and many of them follow it with a tour of their own new listings and MLS properties.

In markets where relocation of people from other cities is an important part of the business, sales meetings may be scheduled for Friday because earlier days of the week are times of most intense sales action. Friday meetings in these firms focus on what's been accomplished during the week and what salespeople's work plans are for the weekend, when local prospects are active.

A number of firms meet twice a week for shorter periods. They say this routine is important to keeping up with their particular market. A few also add a third group session, going on caravan independent of meetings.

The growth of Multiple Listing Service has perhaps had more to do with cutting down on the frequency of sales meetings than any other single factor. This service effectively distributes information between the brokers in markets that offer what is termed "a community of interest." The service saves many hours' time and miles of travel for individual salespeople to acquaint themselves with listings of brokers in adjoining communities that offer similar services and lifestyles. The time thus saved can be put to good use in the home firm, strengthening its listing and sales. The overall result is better service to the buying and selling public.

HOUR OF THE DAY

An early hour seems best for most REALTORS® to schedule meetings for single or branch office meetings. Whether they use the office facilities or meet away from the place of business, getting the group together early in the day works best for two reasons. First, everyone is fresh and free of pressures of appointments and other work to be done. Second, buyers and sellers are less likely to try to reach salespeople at an early hour with either telephone calls or personal visits.

Some firms that have saleswomen with young, school age children say this does not affect their meeting time; others report they feel obliged to set the meeting time a little later to accommodate these family responsibilities. It appears to be a matter of management's knowing its particular situation, what will work and what won't.

Whatever the hour, announce it well in advance, telling not only when the meeting will commence but when it is scheduled to finish. This allows the sales staff to schedule the rest of that working day around the meeting time.

Firms that have multiple branches and a structured series of sales meetings that involve part of the staff at some and the entire organization at others still tend to have local office meetings at the same hour as single-office companies. Their other meetings may substitute for one of the regular weekly sales meetings of the local office staff or they may be held at another hour, depending on who is invited to participate and the length of the meeting. Many large firms call all their salespeople together once a month or once a quarter for sessions that run from a half to a full day.

SHOULD ANYONE LEAVE THE MEETING?

Many brokers believe no salesperson should ever leave a meeting. Their conviction is based on the concept that education is the source of their livelihood and sales meetings are where they are educated; also that if one person leaves, others may also and the meeting can degenerate into a series of interruptions. Since you can't have rules under an independent contractor relationship, this is hard to achieve. As stated earlier, if your meetings provide salespeople material they can use as soon as the meeting ends, they'll be there to get it and will stay on to the end if at all possible.

WHAT ABOUT LATE ARRIVALS?

No one seems to have solved this one yet.

A variety of techniques are used to discourage and even embarrass latecomers but they all result in interruptions to the flow of the meeting. Some sales managers make it a point to draw attention to latecomers as they enter the room. Others make their point if a latecomer asks a question that was answered earlier. To his embarrassment and regret, he is told that the topic has already been discussed. Period. But both these approaches to the latecomer problem are on the negative side.

A more positive approach is suggested by firms with the best record of on-time attendance. They stress the importance of discussing sales meetings with people before they affiliate with the firm, emphasizing management's belief that it is important for salespeople to be prompt, to stay for the entire meeting and how everyone benefits by doing so. This advance discussion seems to work well. Several firms report that the attendance patterns and enthusiasm of new affiliates gradually brings about a change in the few oldtimers who were late or absent.

How a meeting agenda is arranged can also have a beneficial effect on getting people there on time. If some of the most important announcements are made at the beginning and not repeated later, it's amazing how prompt people are.

DURATION OF THE MEETING

The cliché that the mind can absorb only as long as the seat can endure certainly applies to sales meetings.

Be well prepared, have an agenda, keep to it and dismiss the group promptly. Many sales meetings are scheduled to last an hour. Some firms say they accomplish what they want to in a half hour; others say they need an hour and a half. Generalizations are never realistic but the belief that an hour is as long as you can hold people's attention is widely accepted as practical.

Meeting length varies with what you want to accomplish. If meetings are for the fast exchange of information and do not get into training or retraining, it's likely less time is needed. But if training and things like role play are involved, a full hour can be chockfull of useful material.

Seminars, general sales meetings and other major events that cover a half or a full day are planned to include breaks for refreshments or meals. Even these sessions should not run more than a hour and a half without a break that allows people to get up and move about.

Communications specialists say the average rate of speaking is 125 words a minute. The human mind can absorb facts at four times that speed. So when a manager thinks he'll fill time by speaking more slowly, he is in effect planning to lose his audience. Better by far, say the experts, to end a meeting ahead of time than to slow down its tempo. People will remember well the person who dismissed them early, especially if the meeting has provided some new information or a new skill they're anxious to use as quickly as possible.

Set the meeting hour and the time it will end. Making this a part of your preparation can lead to the sales staff setting up their day more efficiently.

NEED FOR FLEXIBILITY

Throughout all the foregoing steps in handling logistics for a single meeting or a series of them, the flexible, creative manager will find himself making changes now and then.

For example, if the local Board announces the showing of a film or the availability of a speaker on a topic of general interest to members, you may decide to forego a scheduled meeting and encourage people to attend the Board function instead. Or you may reduce the length of a regular meeting, confining it to the exchange of listing and sales data which might be covered in about a quarter of the regular meeting time.

You are now ready to communicate the concepts, information and ideas to the group. You are anxious to hear their response and input. When you combine the two, you have truly successful group communication.

CHAPTER 5

Group communication

LEARNING TO COMMUNICATE

This whole book is about communications. That's what sales meetings are all about. But certain aspects of the art of good communications merit special emphasis because they are a manager's challenge and his opportunity. If he can convey an idea in his own words with the force of his own personality behind it, he is a far stronger leader than if he relies on the spoken or written words of another.

There is no such thing as perfect communication any more than there is perfect knowledge. Both are desirable but unattainable because the human mind is imperfect. But when you can communicate what you know in the best way you know how, aware that what you are saying is being heard and understood, you are well on the way to having a fine meeting.

Knowing the right word to use makes communication a pleasure, whether it is the way a salesperson describes a property to someone calling in response to a classified ad or tells a prospect about the community in which he is thinking of investing in property or the way you tell your staff how to do a job well. When one knows the right words to use, he uses them comfortably and effectively.

One of the best communicators in the English speaking world today, Edwin Newman of NBC, has written two books on the subject. His first, *Strictly Speaking*,[1] makes the reader conscious of how we twist and torture English when the use of simple words, stated clearly, would convey our message more effectively. The book is written in a way that makes good language fun and makes fun of bad language.

Newman points out that there are fashion fads in words just as there are in clothing and they can be a very poor fit indeed when a speaker is trying to cover a point.

In recent years the English speaking world in America has been over-burdened with the phrase "Y'know." In the world of communication this is called an articulated pause. Why, if the person speaking expects his listener to know, is he telling him? "Er" and "Ah" are also articulated pauses but do not seem quite as offensive. Not quite. In this noisy world it would be a welcome relief if there were a few *silent* pauses, allowing the listener to absorb what has just been said and the speaker to give a little thought to what has been asked and what his response will be.

DO YOU KNOW WHAT YOU'RE SAYING?

Very few of us are aware of our speech habits. There's a good, easy and relatively inexpensive way to discover how we sound to others. Tape recorders are available everywhere today. Get one and use it to rehearse what you want to say at your next sales meeting. Speak in your natural voice, using words you use every day. Then play it back and listen to how you sound to other people. It can be quite a shock but it will all be very private. Keep doing this for a couple of weeks and you'll probably be pleased to hear that you're correcting some bad speech habits, altering the tone of your voice and, on the whole, coming across as a better-sounding speaker.

(The same technique can be used by your salespeople. Tape recorders can be hooked into the phone at their desk to record their side of phone conversations. Then they can play them back to themselves, listening to how they sound to callers inquiring about properties, dealing with listing owners and handling calls with buyers and others involved in daily negotiations.)

ASSUME NOTHING

Gilbert Highet, writing in *The Immortal Profession*,[2] in which he reflects on his long teaching career, says, "It is our duty to assume that nothing is known, and to explain everything clearly and without condescension. . . . We must always watch our pupils, always striving to discern their interest or lack of interest. By their faces one can tell whether they are following or not."

Highet's essays also reveal how teaching (like real estate) has changed over the years and how important it is to be flexible, ready to adapt to expanding knowledge and always alert to new solutions to old problems.

Recently a college alumnus returned to his alma mater for a 25th reunion. Pausing to renew acquaintance with a favorite professor, he glanced down at the desk and saw a set of examination questions identical to a test he'd been given a quarter century earlier. "Isn't that the same exam you gave me when I was a student?" he asked. "Yes," replied the professor, "but the answers are different today."

This same kind of flexibility is found in Winston Churchill's memoirs which reveal that, despite his vast knowledge of history and more than 50 years' experience in world affairs, he never found a permanent answer to any problem. He could produce only temporary solutions and hope for the best.

Real estate changes along with everything else. Ask anyone who was in the business at mid-century and he will recite battle stories of how it was "back then." Today's smart manager will listen to how it was, knows how it is today and does everything he can to anticipate how it's going to be a year or ten years hence. And if he is able to communicate that knowledge along with his enthusiasm for keeping ahead of the competition he will attract and keep good people.

THE COMPETITION FOR PEOPLE'S ATTENTION

In the years approaching the close of the twentieth century the whole world is being exposed to communications. No one can escape them. They are all fascinating, from earliest Egyptian hieroglyphics to communication satellites. Everyone is bombarded with messages from morning till night.

The very density of modern communications complicates the task of getting and holding the attention of the people to whom we have something *special* to say, something we want them to hold in their minds as they move about in today's cacaphony of competing sounds.

When we are able to communicate successfully our good communications will show up in the bottom line of the business. It's important for today's sales manager to become such a skillful communicator that he is sure what happens in his sales meetings will go far toward producing the results he wants.

It's not easy but it is possible. Understanding some of the basic communication techniques and then putting them into practice in one's own way is sure to help.

FOUR COMMUNICATION TECHNIQUES

The sales manager of one eminently successful firm uses four techniques.

Telling
Selling
Joining
Mutuality of interest.

Telling

The *telling* technique is used when what is being talked about is not open to debate. Topics that relate to company policy and established company procedures are reviewed in a telling manner. There ought to be less *telling* than any of the four techniques in today's sales meetings. A lot of the telling is handled in preliminary interviews with prospective sales associates as you outline how your business is conducted and the framework within which work is done by your sales staff.

If you suspect you are doing too much *telling* in your meetings, ask yourself "Did I *tell* instead of *sell?*" *Telling* is much less effective than *selling*.

Selling

Selling is the technique you can use to show salespeople how they will benefit by following procedures, supplying information the company needs for productive record keeping, accepting floor time, working harder to get listings, make sales or win contests. The *selling* technique can be your best means of communicating with your staff either in sales meetings or one-to-one consultations.

Joining

Joining technique is the approach to use to convey the team concept, to show how everybody working together benefits as individuals while they help others. Topics discussed in a *joining* technique stress the *we* and avoid *I* and *you*, whether in a selling or telling way.

Mutuality of interest

Mutuality of interest is strong in conveying your company's concepts where you are dealing with independent contractors.

The word "independent" harbors the threat of a negative concept in even the best of such relationships. Misuse of the word
has been known to result in salespeople becoming *too* independent for their own good. When you are skilled in presenting
topics in such a way that they prove to be mutually beneficial,
your relationship with your staff will be healthy.

UPWARD COMMUNICATION

The concept of upward communication, important to this business, can be strengthened by having everyone participate in
meetings as much as possible. This is good, practical evidence to
the sales staff that you want—indeed need—to hear what they
have to say.

"No public relations department has ever been able to bring
the outside to top management," said Peter Drucker in a recent
Wall Street Journal interview. Drucker asserted that top management has to get out and hear for themselves but that very few
do even a minimal amount of this. Real estate firms where the
owner or sales manager sells have this advantage over others.
When they do not, they have to rely on the sales staff to bring the
information in to them. Some of it comes in one-to-one conversations but a great deal of it can come in sales meetings.

Who but salespeople can bring in up-to-the-minute reports on
what's being said by both sellers and buyers, general "street
intelligence" like clues to a tightening or easing of the mortgage
market and all the other trends they pick up every day? Sure,
you hear some of these things but you cannot be everywhere
every day. When information of this kind is part of a sales meeting, the salespeople hear it all together. Then, if it eventually
affects company plans or policy the whole group has a better
understanding of what caused the change.

Upward communication is important for other reasons, too. It
indicates to the staff that you care about what they think and
what they know about the market, and that communication
moves in both directions in a healthy, open exchange. It's important to the concept of team effort so necessary to the success of a
brokerage firm. It means that secrecy has no place in the operation of the business.

GETTING EVERYONE TO COMMUNICATE

As you plan, include notes of how staff can be encouraged to participate all through the meeting, how you will illustrate salient
points, stimulate questions and answers and what to listen and
watch for as the meeting moves along.

Even when you play a strong *telling* role in a meeting, the sales staff should be given an opportunity to express their opinions, give their reactions. This is important to them and helps prevent the feeling that they're called together once a week to listen to a lecture.

Remember the complaints: *"The broker (or sales manager) does almost all the talking."* And, *"The broker ramrods his decisions through without asking for our reactions, much less welcoming our opinions and ideas."*

George M. Prince, renowned for his work in group problem-solving, writing in *The Practice of Creativity*,[3] says "There are appropriate roles for each participant in a meeting. If these are understood and adhered to, the probability of success can be substantially increased.

"In traditional meetings each participant operates at two different levels. At one level he recognizes the organization of the meeting. He assumes that the (chairman) is in charge and that he himself is there to help solve someone else's problem. There are three recognizable roles here: leader, expert, participant."

Prince explains the second level as the one where the participant shifts from one role to another as he feels the need, whether to contribute an idea, a criticism or a dissertation.

SOME BEHAVIORAL PROBLEMS

The roles in a real estate sales meeting are more clearly defined than they are in many other kinds of meetings but some of the same behavioral problems work against the meeting's probability of success. For example, there is a high level of antagonism toward ideas. People have a strong identity with their own ideas and any antagonism toward them is seen as a personal attack. The extent and effects of these attacks are remarkable.

Prince reports an experiment he conducted in an attempt to measure the effect of seemingly mild antagonism. While the test was not considered definitive it did reveal scientific proof that everyone responds actively to antagonism. Statements made to the subject ranged from saying in a quiet voice, "I am not upset or anything, but I am going to gently slap your arm," to responding to the subject's idea with the familiar cliché, "I hate to be negative *but*," and then finding fault with what the subject had just said. The subject remained outwardly calm but the electrode's point moved slightly in the first instance and sharply at the negative statement.

If you bear in mind the complaints listed in Chapter 1, you will realize that they and all the other difficulties in the group tend to make the meeting a collection of competing individuals instead of a team.

Indeed, you are one of the competing individuals. You are up front, leading the group. Chances are very good that every one of the salespeople really believes he would be doing a better job if he were up there!

It is important to do all you can to mitigate this feeling. You can do this by engaging the capabilities of each person in the meeting, using its collective strength to achieve whatever the objective of the meeting is, doing it in such a way that it does not arouse resentment.

"But I have ideas, too," you protest. "Isn't it more constructive for me to put them into the pot?"

Yes and no.

Ideas from the sales staff should be given first priority. You should support them, restating them to make certain you understand them thoroughly and whenever possible building on them or strengthening them in whatever way you can. After the salespeople's ideas are contributed and developed, it is time for you to introduce your own. It is to be hoped that by then some of your ideas will already have been contributed from the group.

No meeting can afford to lose anybody's ideas. The sequence in which you present your ideas is what's important. It's the most natural thing in the world that when a sales manager contributes *his* ideas first, he unconsciously favors them. The rest of the people in the meeting are sensitive to this and will resent it, sometimes to the point of tuning out the whole meeting. When this happens, the whole meeting is lost for those people and their relationship to the sales manager is impaired for an even longer time.

But there are times when your ideas are needed. They should be offered when there is no other action or when possible solutions are being sought and the group is actually looking to management for guidance.

COMMUNICATION THROUGH LISTENING

Restating ideas contributed by the staff people proves to them that you have not only listened to what they are saying but that you understand. When you participate by listening you are, in effect, saying to your people, "I am here to listen to what you have in mind and to help build on your thoughts. I am not here to make judgments." Such a posture both satisfies the staff and creates an atmosphere where all ideas are assumed worthy of consideration by the group.

HOW TO HANDLE "BAD" HUMOR

There's nothing as destructive to a person's morale as having his ideas laughed at or scorned. It's the leader's job to search for value in any idea a salesperson offers in the meeting. For example, an inexperienced person may come up with a totally new concept of telephone canvassing. The rest of the group may be so scornful of it that they burst into spontaneous laughter, whereupon the new salesperson retreats with an offhand, "I wasn't really serious about that." But the skillful meeting leader doesn't let it go at that. He asks some questions, probing for an emerging idea that will prove useful and practical. When a leader misses such an opportunity the whole team may have tossed away an idea worth many dollars to everyone, while the person who offered it may be turned off from participating in the rest of that meeting and for weeks afterward.

KEEPING COMMUNICATION POSITIVE

When a member of the meeting is known for negative reactions to almost any idea put forth, it can be a challenge to handle him judiciously. Someone like this often has another bad trait—voicing his negative reaction before anyone else has had a chance to speak. How can you cope with this double problem?

Experience suggests two methods. In the first, the moment that person's hand is raised to indicate he wants to speak, take it out of a negative situation by responding, "Let's hear what you *like* about this idea, Dick." And when Dick's hand goes up too often or if he starts to speak without being recognized, the response can be, "We've heard your reactions several times today, Dick. Now let's move on around the room and let each person offer his opinion."

When you do this, you accomplish two things: You let everyone in the room know you're aware of Dick's negativism and his tendency to take more than a fair share of the meeting time; and you give everybody in the room a lesson in how to handle such a person tactfully without putting him on the defensive.

COMMUNICATING THE OBJECTIVE

Sales meetings aren't sermons but expressing sales meeting objectives can be likened to a sermon in terms of communication. In the words of a professor teaching a group of seminary students the basics of sermon preparation, it goes this way:

"First you tell them what you're going to tell them.
Then you tell them.
Then you tell them what you've just told them."

It is at the beginning of the meeting that you must get the attention of your people. In a well-stated objective, "Tell them what you are going to tell them." If the objective is "How We Can Get More Listings" simply reading that statement may be sufficient introduction. Then it's followed by a couple of sentences telling how the objective will be pursued later in the meeting and what you want the salespeople to be prepared to start doing after the meeting is over.

Keep it brief. Use action words. (*Canvass. Call. Contact.*) This is not the time to go into details. They will come in the second phase of the meeting's objective, the "then you tell them" portion.

Finally, after the group has participated in the listening, telling, discussion, role play and whatever other means you have prepared for the main part of the meeting, "tell them what you've just told them."

It's communications, communications, communications all the way whether the staff is being told, sold, asked to join a team effort or being appealed to on the basis of a mutuality of interest. It will succeed best when there is total communication—both to and from management.

COMMUNICATING THE WEEK'S ACTION

Staff reports are put first on the agenda of many real estate sales meetings. Among the reasons given for this "order of business" are that it gets the staff in a participating frame of mind at the beginning of the meeting, it helps with the problem of getting people there on time and these details then become part of the general frame of reference for the rest of the session.

Everybody participates. Whether a salesperson has a new listing he wants to tell about or a sale closed about which the rest of the staff hasn't heard, this is his moment of glory. How he communicates to the rest of the group is important. Giving his fellow salespeople details of a new listing can be a rehearsal of what he'll tell prospects or REALTORS® from other firms when they inquire as a result of ads or the MLS listing. Listen carefully to these staff presentations and ask questions in such a way that important information not included by the salesperson can be added. Thus, a manager skilled in communications can use even the briefest moments of a meeting to help salespeople improve *their* communication skills. What they learn to say clearly to their peers they will say just as clearly and more naturally to the public later.

Details of sales for the past week communicates to everyone the prices being realized in the market at the moment, facts that will be useful to all of them in terms of both the immediate market and the general trend. Other information of value to the whole staff includes the names of both buyers and sellers, whether buyers are new to the area and will have friends who may wish to move into the area or if the sellers are leaving the area or are in the market for another property. Mortgage information may suggest new sources of financing, a change in money rates or some other factor that could influence other sales in the week ahead.

Through this whole segment of the meeting, be alert to both the news being communicated and the skill the staff has or needs. Make note of it.

COMMUNICATING PRAISE

While we live with the cliché that *money talks*, management understands the importance of sincere thanks for a job well done. Commissions are of prime importance. Praise is a close second. Very few real estate sales are the result of anything but good, hard work. Whether the salesperson is the top person on the staff, a middle producer or someone just getting started, he needs praise in addition to payment. (Remember the Maslow hierarchy of needs.) Sales meetings are the best place for praise. Give it as sales are reported.

The sales manager who has good upward communication from the staff will know just what kind of effort each sale required. As he compliments the salesperson he has a fine opportunity to share a few of the details with everybody in the meeting.

If the sale was made by a top producer, for example, take the opportunity to point out how well this person organizes his time or how it may seem to others that sales come his way with what appears to be less effort than others put out but how long he worked to develop the skill needed to work well with people.

For the middle producer, this sale may be his first since attending a Marketing Institute course. Tell how he used some of the negotiating skills he learned at the course. For the beginning salesperson, the compliment can be given with the expressed belief that it marks an important beginning, to be followed by a long series of successful sales.

Sometimes applause will be spontaneous. Suggest it for everyone. This is a time when "equal treatment" is important to the ego of everyone who's being paid. Interestingly, applause of the peer group may be more important to the top person than to the newcomer. The latter will be excited at making his first sale and may not notice applause as much as an experienced associate who, rightly or wrongly, may have come to think he is taken too much for granted.

Do not lose sight of one important point. Commissions are compensation for work done. They are not rewards in the context of a prize or a special company bonus or some other form of remuneration. A broker pays his independent contractors a stipulated percentage as their share of the whole commission. Announcing the sale allows you to express the firm's gratitude for his being part of a team effort, adding to the benefits shared by all.

COMMUNICATING REWARDS

Contests and games need the stimulation of good communication from the announcement to the finish. Sales meetings are used to keep the enthusiasm up as sales contests or games move along, regardless of how well they're posted and promoted in the office on a daily basis. Salespeople enjoy these special competitive drives. A minute or two on a meeting agenda gives the chance to tell who's doing well at the moment, who's in the lead, who's improving most from the last week's place and what kind of effort will be needed to bring the contest to a strong finish.

OTHER KINDS OF RECOGNITION

That idea bank of clippings will include news items of salespeople's part in local events and civic and business affairs. Warm praise encourages those who deserve it and may stimulate others to develop interests and activities beyond their work. Whether these activities have a direct bearing on the business or not, there is at least an indirect public relations benefit when people affiliated with the firm are active in the community.

After the meeting, these news clippings can go up on the office bulletin board for all to read at their leisure.

COMMUNICATION OF SPECIAL PROBLEMS

The sample agenda in Chapter 3 allots some time to salespeople's problem transactions, their needs for specific kinds of properties and anything else that relates to the immediate market where the whole staff can offer help.

A problem listing, nearing its expiration date, may be priced too high. The salesperson asks for ideas on how to approach the owner with a realistic price change suggestion. As you listen to what the staff is saying you are also busy dredging up from memory a similar situation from the past. If you can recall which salesperson was involved ask that person to tell how it was handled and why he believes it worked.

Many commercial exchange transactions have their origins in sales meetings where the needs and wants of buyers and sellers are discussed. One person has a client with an income property he wants to trade up to a bigger one; another may have just heard about a building big enough to satisfy the first person's client but that owner also wants to sell some vacant land because he's retiring and leaving the community. Then somebody else recalls talking to an investor looking for vacant land awhile back. Out of that assortment of properties the sales manager recognizes the possibilities of a series of exchanges. He guides the talk so the group begins to see it, too. No more meeting time is devoted to the subject but the three salespeople and the sales manager pursue the course of action immediately after the meeting.

Such a forum of ideas provides the setting for many of the best exchanges in the business. After all, regional and national meetings are held by investment brokers for this purpose. And when the sales staff knows the discussion period offers such opportunities to participate, even the most experienced senior staff people are more likely to be there.

GOOD COMMUNICATION PAYS DOUBLE BENEFITS

Skillful use of good communication techniques in your meetings not only helps convey your telling or selling message but also exposes salespeople to practices they can use later in their work.

Whenever you stop to explain the meaning of a term that may be new to the staff you are also suggesting the need to make everything clear to everyone. Later, those salespeople making a listing presentation or working with prospective buyers are less apt to use unfamiliar words or terms without explaining them.

It's easy to use trade shorthand like "down" when "down payment" is being discussed. The prospect may understand "down." But if the salesperson continues to use words and terms that are foreign to the listener he may nod in agreement when he doesn't understand at all. Why? Because it's a natural human trait to not want to admit a lack of knowledge. It's up to the salesperson to sense his listener's confusion and take care to explain things fully as he goes along. The everyday language of real estate is as difficult to a doctor as his medical jargon is to a real estate person who goes to him for treatment. The difference in the situations is that the doctor won't buy what he doesn't understand.

ROLE PLAY

Role play as a teaching/learning/practice medium in real estate selling enjoys the enthusiastic acceptance of some, occasional use by others and the absolute disdain of a few.

At its best, role play offers salespeople an opportunity to practice what they have learned and a chance to learn new skills and techniques either by participating or by watching others in a peer setting. It offers all these advantages in a situation that costs them no more than the meeting time it takes, at absolutely no risk of losing a listing or a sale and the commission that goes with them. Without that valuable role play the risk of losing listings and sales is greater and, of course, defeat is harder to accept when it costs money.

Role play is introduced here because it is an important part of group communications in so many real estate sales organizations today. It is treated more fully in Appendix B where a variety of situations and general instructions are given for each type.

REALTORS® who have tried role play with what they consider little or no success may have negative reactions that stem from a bruised ego because they think they are the only ones who know how to do things well. In these cases, if role play develops techniques and responses the manager isn't familiar with, it's destructive to his ego. Such a person has to decide whether his ego is more important than his salespeople's and whether ego matters more than the bottom line of the profit and loss statement. Role play can be a very successful technique. Try it. You'll like it.

When salespeople are reluctant to participate, find out why. Perhaps the experienced ones may veto the idea, thinking they have nothing to learn (ego again) while new salespeople may be yearning to have a try at it. This is where upward communication from the whole staff is important and where you are challenged to communicate through a selling technique.

---

1. Newman, *Strictly Speaking.*
2. Highet, *The Immortal Profession.*
3. Prince, *The Practice of Creativity.*

CHAPTER 6

Conducting the meeting

CONDUCTING MEETINGS

There are no unmanageable sales meetings. There are only managers who don't know how to manage meetings. An exaggeration? Perhaps. But it will stand for all practical purposes.

A sales manager who has difficulty getting order and keeping it is a person who really doesn't *expect* order. His futility and frustration can be replaced with authority and confidence.

Salespeople get YOU when they associate with the firm. The YOU who is sales manager will play an important role in their deciding to stay or to move on to another organization.

Conducting the sales meeting becomes the bottom line of all the thought, preparation of materials and agenda, the logistics that lead up to the meeting. Now your challenge is to control the direction a meeting takes, making sure it comes as close as possible to reaching the preconceived objective.

Some professionals believe that control of a meeting starts with who is invited to attend. If the room holds a mix of people not all of whom stand to gain by what's on the program, even one or two who are bored can "take it away" from the leader. Some do it with long joke sessions, others by open yawning or squirming to show they're bored. Bored people can distract listeners without ever opening their mouths. To those who believe this will happen, the answer is to ask only those who will benefit by being there, then to make sure everyone can take away something that will be immediate help in his work.

Remember the real estate cliché, you can't make them come and you can't make them listen!

PUNCTUALITY

Remember also the complaint: *"We never start on time, never get out on time."*

There's a tradition in England that is called "theatrical margin" which by unspoken rule states that if a show is to start at 8:30 there is neither intention or expectation that it will do so. Instead, the overture will sound precisely seven minutes after the time stated on the ticket. The show is not seven minutes late in getting started. It is right on the button. All cues are attuned to the actual 8:37 starting time. The custom was begun centuries ago to accommodate latecomers.

Sales meetings are a different matter. People do not attend to be entertained or amused. People come to sales meetings to be informed, to be helped and to be stimulated, expecting to leave the meeting self-motivated to do a better job.

Sales meetings that start late are as welcome as a blindfold at a gaming table. It's frustrating, disappointing and discouraging to be penalized for promptness. That, in effect, is what happens when a meeting starts late. The people who were on time are penalized and minutes are stolen from their day because of poor planning. It's not the fault of the tardy ones when a meeting starts late. It's the fault of the person running the meeting.

When a meeting is delayed "until a few more people get here," the clear message is that promptness doesn't pay but tardiness does. Those who came on time, ready to participate, often become so resentful of delays that they are tuned out of the whole meeting, negating all the planning and preparation a manager has put into it.

It is far better to close a meeting two minutes early than to start it two minutes late.

Start on the dot no matter who's missing. Reward promptness by putting important things or "goodies" at the beginning.

The lively, creative topics that require mental energy and clear heads move along better early in the meeting. New listings, changes in interest rates, completed sales, changes in company policy, all rate high on such a list.

Promptness can also be rewarded with a touch of fun and games. A quick look for dollar bills taped to the bottom of chairs or a drawing for dinner for two at a popular restaurant are a couple of suggestions that come to mind. Only those in the room at the appointed time (maybe five minutes before starting time) can participate.

PRE-MEETING TREATS

The congeniality of pre-meeting treats like coffee and sweet rolls helps insure promptness in some organizations. When refreshments are served at the office, some brokers clear away all the food service just ahead of starting time. Those who don't get there ahead of time miss out on the treat.

LATECOMERS, EARLY LEAVERS

Some firms strongly discourage coming to a meeting late or leaving early. Their belief is that if one person is allowed the privilege, everyone is, resulting in partial participation for some of the people, interruption of the whole group and a manager who's not sure who was there for what part of the meeting.

These firms claim that their people soon learn to schedule their work *around* the meeting time just as carefully as they book appointments for listing and sales work that are free of conflict. If meetings are interesting enough, people will be there on time and stay through to the close.

GETTING STARTED

Some managers find it awkward to open a meeting. It can be quite simple. Silence impels attention. Rap for attention, announce the opening of the meeting then with a confident smile, wait for silence. Show no trace of annoyance. Say nothing more. See how eloquent a pleasant, expectant silence can be. In the space of 40 seconds the group will be silent. In less than a minute the manager has set the tone for the whole meeting: smiling attention.

If, on the other hand, an effort is made to force attention, the manager is setting himself against the others. It will be him against the group for the duration of that meeting, a negative tone from the beginning.

Using a bell or gavel with the force of a pile driver antagonizes the audience. This seems to say, "Boy, am I going to have trouble this morning!" That manager expects trouble. He gets it.

Both the positive and negative reactions described above are instinctive.

MOVING ALONG

Having got the salespeople's attention, the next challenge is to hold it, to stimulate their participation in the meeting and keep the whole thing moving along on schedule.

Some of the skills this requires include the following.

Knowing how to draw people out.
Knowing how to silence the overly talkative.
Knowing how to move negative thinkers a few degrees toward the positive.
Knowing how to summarize what's been said.

If you're weak in any of the above skills, substitute the word "learning" for knowing.

GENERATING PARTICIPATION

In a well run meeting, most of the people will be silent most of the time. It's just simple, good arithmetic—only one person can (or should) be talking at any time. With even 100 percent participation each person will have just so many chances to express an opinion or put forth an idea. What matters is the *reason* for silence.

The first step toward drawing people out is to be aware of the reasons for their silence.

If people are quiet because they agree with what's being said or because they have nothing important to contribute or if they are inclined to wait and hear more before they say anything, it need not be a special concern to the leader.

When they are silent because of diffidence or hostility, it is important to do something about it. The silence of diffidence may reflect the person who, though he has a valuable contribution to make, may be nervous about speaking and takes the easy way out, saying nothing. The sales manager who takes the trouble to really know his people will spot this trait and work gently to encourage the shy person to express himself. Encouragement needn't take the form of agreement or adulation but merely reflect pleasure at that person's participation.

Hostility is another matter. It doesn't reflect a hostility to *ideas* but to the manager or the meeting or the process by which decisions are reached. One clue to hostile silence is a person's seeming detachment from the whole proceedings. It reflects some feeling of affront. The meeting is not the place to probe this but it ought to be pursued as quickly as possible afterwards. That person has something important to say and the sooner he says it the better for the manager and the whole firm.

ENCOURAGING NEWCOMERS

Inexperienced salespeople, full of enthusiasm to share whatever comes into their heads, may incur the displeasure of older staff members. Both the action and the reaction are perfectly normal. But if it is allowed to get out of hand, to reach the point where senior staff people let it be known that newcomers aren't making any contribution, the meeting is weakened and seeds of hostility are sown.

Listen, observe and move in to handle the situation before it goes too far. Take pains to commend newcomers for useful ideas and for exploring new approaches to old problems. This satisfies them and is a psychological prod to other staff to do likewise.

Newcomers get a lift from seemingly small gestures like a manager writing down an idea they've just contributed or referring back to it later in the meeting.

AVOIDING DIALOGUES

Sales meetings are not the place for *continuing* dialogues between managers and salespeople. They are the place for discussion and debate, even for a clash of ideas. Guide the exchange of ideas or a debate between salespeople; probe, stimulate and occasionally summarize but never dominate a discussion. Keep the meeting focused on ideas and away from personalities.

When things begin to heat up too much between individuals, widen the discussion. Bring in another person, using the simple technique of asking a neutral question that requires a factual answer. Then summarize and move on to the next item on the agenda. For example, salesperson Jim says, "I think we should spend some money on radio ads." Salesperson Joe retorts, "Naw. We tried that two years ago and it was a bust." You know these two people are basically antagonistic to each other, so you intervene with, "Well, Joe, the market situation is far different now, isn't it? Let's get some figures from local stations on their best rush hour talk shows. Then we'll discuss at next week's meeting what radio might do for us this year. Now, let's move on to our next item."

MURPHY'S LAW

Despite the most careful preparation, things go awry in every meeting. A situation called Murphy's Law develops (Murphy's assumption was that anything that can go wrong probably will) and it will appear to a manager that he needs the wisdom of Solomon and the patience of Job.

Topics never dreamed of are introduced by the salespeople. Certain people who talk too much or too often or always negatively will add pressures to your task, and sometimes a real revolt is tossed in, like a giant firecracker, taking the meeting far off its target. How can these situations and people be handled discreetly without closing off the open communication you need?

WHEN ONE PERSON TALKS TOO MUCH

Controlling the garrulous can be a tough challenge. (Complaint: *One salesperson is allowed to dominate the meeting whenever the broker asks for staff opinions or ideas.*) People of this nature are glad that someone else has assembled an audience for them and are quick to use the group as the object of their superior knowledge and wisdom.

When someone in the meeting has a habit of taking a long time to say very little he can sometimes be dealt with by the simple statement that there is much to be covered in a limited time and thus not enough time for prolonged statements. If this doesn't work, you can stop him in full flight by interrupting, repeating a statement the "over-talker" has just made and passing that statement along to someone else in the room for confirmation or comment. "Fine, George. I think we all agree that it's best to have a couple seated facing you when you're making a listing presentation. Sue, do you have anything to add to that?" It won't matter to the talker *where* you break into his recital; it will matter a lot to the rest of the people *that* you break in somewhere—*anywhere*—and give everyone else a chance to participate.

When the problem is a person who's at the ready to answer every call for participation, another tactic has proved workable. Look at another person as you ask for response, visually cutting off the person who dominates the meeting. Or set up a ground rule that answers will be given in rotation around the group. Then if the over-eager one still gets a wedge in, take it away from him by stating firmly that he has contributed quite a lot to the meeting thus far and it's now time to listen to the others.

HANDLING THE NEGATIVE ONES

Real estate sales, like all the rest of the world, is burdened with what seems more than its fair share of people who believe "it ain't gonna work." These negative souls will find reasons why the sky will fall on every project suggested, every new idea developed. (They don't really like other people, so why should they like other people's ideas?) Whatever the technique or topic being discussed, negative people will have a list of reasons to squelch it. If someone of this nature gets control of the meeting it is in danger of becoming sterile because nobody likes to have his opinions or ideas ridiculed.

You have a double challenge in this situation. You must first and most importantly nurture the ego of the person who contributed the positive idea, then discourage the squelcher as sharply as possible. A genuinely skillful manager can even challenge the negative person to produce a better idea on the spot or to tell what he *likes* about what has just been suggested. If you can put down the squelcher and lead the others to help build the original suggestion into something that will work, you've achieved a victory and the staff will recognize it.

COPING WITH REVOLT

It always comes as a shock to realize that communications with the group have not been good; it's a worse shock when it's communicated by an open revolt in a sales meeting.

There is no pat formula for dealing with revolt but there are ways to be prepared for it by knowing how to proceed when it happens.

Some revolts can be handled on the spot. Others require listening and reacting at the moment, to be followed by further discussion at a later meeting or in another setting.

Mild forms of revolt can be handled fairly by keeping the dissenters coming toward you, asking them to restate their complaints, absorbing blows from them as they would from an irate customer, treating the situation like a legitimate objection in a sales situation. People loosen up when they're being listened to. Such a sequence might go something like the following.

> *Listen*—hear them out, listening for a point on which management is in agreement. Interrupt at this point, restating the complaint and
> *Agree*—with a specific point, then move to
> *Examine the facts*—if there are not enough facts available on their side, present management's, asking them all to consider and
> *Discuss positively*—contributing ideas that will work.
> *Give credit*—for sound ideas.
> *Question*—whether the proposal (or change) applies now for both the company and the sales staff.
> *Summarize*—and give complainers a way to back down gracefully if that's what is needed, or agree to submit the subject for management's consideration and report back at the next meeting.

When the revolt requires more information than is available during the meeting, approach it in another way. Listening is still a primary requisite to skillful handling of the revolt. As soon as enough has been said to supply the clues for further information needed, terminate the discussion by summarizing what's been said, what factual information is missing and finish with a promise to put the topic on the agenda for the next meeting.

For example, what may start out as a discussion of a listing that's about to expire may suddenly explode into accusations that management has cut back on classified ads without advising the sales staff. Management knows better but, rather than argue without facts, the accusations are summarized and a promise made that actual figures for the year to date and the budgeted amount will be brought to the next meeting.

If expenditures are in line with what was budgeted and if the sales staff knew what the budgeted figures were, it will be a relatively simple matter to report these facts. But if market conditions have caused a change in ad plans it will be important to share these facts, too, and explain what is planned for the rest of the year. Failure to have communicated this in advance makes it hard to do in a situation of revolt but offers a chance to admit error graciously.

The subject of a revolt may often mask salespeople's dissatisfaction with something entirely different. Exploratory talks with a few of them after the meeting may disclose the real reason for revolt, perhaps something that wasn't even broached during the meeting.

Whether in a meeting or not, management that keeps salespeople coming toward them, in a positive, permissive atmosphere, is less likely to encounter revolt.

THE SUMMING UP

A good meeting occurs when the group revises, updates and adds to what it knows *as a group*. Summarizing what has taken place in a meeting or a part of a meeting strengthens the team concept. Knowing when to step in and summarize a discussion is important to keeping a meeting on schedule. Knowing how to summarize the achievement of a meeting's total objective helps the group leave in a positive frame of mind.

Summaries combine proof of listening, skill in selecting highlights and the ability to restate them accurately in a few words.

Listen carefully as others speak, making notes of points of emphasis to be used in the summary. When restating the words of others, do it as accurately as possible; then ask the person

quoted if it reflects what he meant to say. Look carefully as he
replies, asking him to state his point if he disagrees with what
was said in summary. This is not just good management, it's
good manners.

Meeting agendas are valuable aids in summarizing the meeting content. They remind the leader how much has been accomplished, highlights of individual achievement and group decisions
to be implemented in the week ahead.

MAKING MEETINGS USEFUL

Antony Jay is chairman of Video Arts, Ltd., London, a company
that is producing a training film on the subject of meetings. Research for the project led Jay to write "How To Run a Meeting,"[1]
which appeared recently in *Harvard Business Review*. In stating
the basic challenge of conducting meetings, Jay says, "Meetings
are *necessary* for all sorts of basic and primitive human reasons,
but they are *useful* only if they are seen by all present to be
getting somewhere—and somewhere they know they could not
have gotten to individually.

"If the (chairman) is to make sure that the meeting achieves
valuable objectives, he will be more effective seeing himself as
the servant of the group rather than as its master. His role then
becomes that of assisting the group toward the best conclusion
or decision in the most efficient manner possible; to interpret
and clarify; to move the discussion forward; and to bring it to a
resolution that everyone understands and accepts as being the
will of the meeting, even if the individuals do not necessarily
agree with it."

Jay goes on to say that once a (sales) staff realizes that the
manager is impelled by his commitment to the common objective, it does not take great force of personality for him to control
the meeting. The effective chairman (manager) can hold a
discussion to the point by indicating that there is no time to
pursue a particular idea now, that there is no time for long
speeches, that the group has to get through one item and on to
the next. He doesn't have to resort to pulling rank.

HOW CAN YOU INDICATE IMPATIENCE?

There are a few physical actions such as leaning forward, fixing
your eyes on the speaker, tensing your muscles, raising your
eyebrows or nodding briefly to show the point is taken. Some
verbal actions are possible, like indicating with the speed, brevity
and finality of your voice that "we have to move along."

HOW CAN YOU ENCOURAGE FURTHER DISCUSSION?

There are converse actions to those just mentioned, like a relaxed expression and voice intonation to show there is time to give further consideration to an idea just presented, encouraging the speaker to go on and develop his point.

After these techniques have been used in a few meetings the staff will understand your nonverbal language. This skill can be used to establish the meeting behavior you want. You will continue to be the servant of the group but, like a mountain guide, you are most familiar with the destination, the best route to take and how long it will take to get there. When you act to speed up the group you are, in a sense, just asking them to walk a little faster, says Jay.

THE AGENDA: AN IMPORTANT PAPER

Some managers circulate a general agenda to their sales staff once a month so they know the kinds of meetings planned and can come prepared to take part. Others distribute agendas in advance only to those who will participate in a structured way— i.e., lead a discussion, participate in role play or give a first person report on how a transaction was handled.

Whether the agenda is distributed to the staff in advance of the meeting, shared with them at the meeting or is the sole possession of the manager, it is a very important piece of paper. It is the manager's guide to what he wants to have happen in the meeting, reminders of how he will emphasize certain points and the time schedule necessary to adhere to in order to keep things moving toward the stated objective.

As a manager follows his prepared agenda and its accompanying timetable he is continually aware of whether the meeting is getting out of hand by dwelling too long on routine items to the exclusion of what he wants the meeting to focus on. Side conversations that start up in the group as listings and sales are discussed can slow down the proceedings. If they are important enough to be talked about they should be shared with the whole group. If they can't be dispatched within the time assigned, it may be worthwhile to postpone detailed discussion to the next meeting, explored later with individual salespeople or assigned to certain salespeople for further study and reporting back at a later meeting. Sometimes one meeting's "sidelines" become another meeting's main topic.

People who are less experienced in planning meetings are more likely to prepare agendas that are too brief or too vague or both. The sample on page 35 is about as brief as an agenda can be

and still be useful as a guide to both topics and timing. People
new to meeting planning will likely want one with more detail,
perhaps including reminders of why certain topics are being
discussed and how and where to work in supplemental materials.

THE "HIDDEN AGENDA"

Listing "any other business" as a standard part of a meeting
agenda is an open invitation to waste time. Jay points out in his
Harvard Business Review article, "All items should be thought
of and thought about in advance if they are to be usefully discussed."

But it is a rare meeting that doesn't require you to exercise
some flexibility in following a prepared agenda. For good and
valid reason you may decide to introduce an extra agenda item.
Salespeople should also be allowed to bring up subjects that are of
new and immediate concern to them. Keeping an agenda flexible
for them is part of the necessary free exchange which is a
strength of a good sales meeting.

"Hidden agenda" items ought to be topics that can be handled
in a straightforward, expeditious way so they do not extend the
meeting beyond announced dismissal time. There is another
caution, that interruptions of this kind can result in a leader
throwing away all his advance work if he lets others take over
the meeting. A well-timed agenda provides some minutes of
leeway. When it appears that unexpected topics require more
time than allotted they should be postponed to a later meeting,
then definitely scheduled for further discussion.

Other concepts of a "hidden agenda" include the items salespeople expect or want to have included in the meeting and the
distracting influence of talk that develops among two or three
people as a meeting progresses.

The first mentioned can be spotted by a manager who is aware
that one (or more) of the salespeople appears to have tuned out
the proceedings. His dilemma is to choose between ignoring this
or interrupting the meeting to explore what's bothering the non-
participant. Ignoring it won't make the problem disappear; it
may result in the salesperson engaging in a silent takeover of the
meeting or starting to converse privately with the person next to
him. Then the manager has lost *two* of the audience. Better by
far to get to that person at the first possible moment with a
query of what is on his mind, then deal with it as expeditiously as
possible or promise to put the subject on the agenda of the following meeting.

Distracting side conversations can be handled by asking
questions like, "Joe, are you saying something we all should
hear?" Or, "Joe, let's hear what you are sharing with Jack if it

relates to what we're talking about." One of two things are likely to happen: Joe *does* have something interesting and pertinent to share and proceeds to tell the group; or he *doesn't* and will quit talking. Either way, the point is made and you stay in control.

USING AN AGENDA

There is a sense of power that accompanies managing a meeting. No matter what fears or uneasiness you have about chairing sales meetings, a certain headiness is natural the first time you take your place in front of the group. It's nothing to be ashamed of but it's the last thing in the world you should nurture. You are not up front to indulge your ego; you're up there to lead the meeting toward achieving its stated objective.

In Jay's words, "If the chairman is to make sure that the meeting achieves valuable objectives, he will be more effective seeing himself as the servant of the group rather than as its master. His role then becomes that of assisting the group toward the best conclusion or decision in the most efficient manner possible: to interpret and clarify; to move the discussion forward; and to bring it to a resolution that everyone understands and accepts as being the will of the meeting, even if the individuals do not necessarily agree with it."

A manager's true source of authority with the staff is the strength of his perceived commitment to the success of the whole group and his skill in guiding them to its achievement. When the whole group participates in the meeting, the manager is not imposing his will or discipline on them. He is acting as their guide as they move from item to item, exploring ideas, holding to the point of discussion and exerting the group's will on those who threaten diversion from the mainstream of thought. An effective leader uses a carefully prepared agenda to hold the meeting to the main objective, leading away from long speeches because of the need to get through one item and on to the next. A strong agenda negates a need for a leader to pull rank. His danger signal should fly when he hears himself talk a lot. He feels strongest when he's busy listening to others.

CHANGING PACE

Albert Einstein once said, "When you sit with a nice girl for two hours, you think it's only a minute. But when you sit on a hot stove for a minute, you think it's two hours. That's relativity."

Management people tend to forget that while they're up front, moving about at their own pace, the audience is seated, expected to remain alert and mentally active throughout the meeting.

Real estate is not sold by people who sit at desks. Real estate salespeople are activists, up-and-out doers. Holding their attention is difficult. Because they are not naturally passive learners, the psychological and physical switch is hard for them to make. They soon become restless and inattentive.

Changes of pace as a meeting progresses are important. They can vary from straight listening, discussion, role play or buzz sessions interspersed with an occasional break to take a stretch. If such breaks are not provided, they'll be taken anyway and will disrupt the meeting.

Even when breaks are provided, watch for signs of fatigue or drowsiness. If the meeting includes a lot of "telling," a change of the rate in speaking sometimes helps.

Research shows that the average rate of speaking is about 125 words per minute. The mind is able to absorb approximately 500 words per minute. This difference can cause a speaker to lose his audience's attention. It would be folly to talk or try to talk at maximum speed. Listeners would be uncomfortable with such a radical change and would lose track of what is being said as they focus on how long the new pace can last. But moderate change of pace is a help.

TECHNIQUES WITH AUDIO/VISUALS

A darkened room is necessary for audio/visuals from a mechanical standpoint but can prove a problem by lulling the audience. One way to overcome this is to choose places where a logical break occurs, turn up the lights and discuss what's been seen. During this break you may choose to go to the front of the room or ask the audience to turn toward you at the back if you are operating the projector from that area. The latter method offers at least a little movement, which may be a welcome change to the viewers.

Participation at this juncture of a meeting is important because the group has been sitting through a "telling" session in a darkened room, perhaps fighting drowsiness despite their interest in the film. Questions like "Jim, how do you think we can use the techniques we've just seen here?" or "Mary, can you see opportunities to try the sales approach just outlined?" can help make materials prepared by outside organizations more personal and so more useful.

Unannounced breaks in the presentation also help keep the audience aware that more such breaks may be coming and they'd best be prepared to participate.

REFRAIN FROM APOLOGIZING

Apologies weaken a meeting. If there is a valid reason for something on the agenda not being included, say so.

"Mr. Soandso was called out of town on an emergency. We'll schedule him at the first available date." That's infinitely better than "It's too bad Mr. Soandso isn't here to speak to us today."

When a manager says, "I'm sorry we're late getting started," he's calling attention to his own weakness. If there is a valid reason, state it. "An emergency at home prevented my getting here on time." If meetings start on time, the staff will accept a genuine emergency. Don't try to fool them.

"We meant to include . . ." indicates incomplete preparation or poor planning. Better to add an upbeat extra to the agenda than to plan for something and then not follow through. Some people might be there because that part of the meeting attracted them. Disappointed, they'll tune out the rest of the session.

"If only we had time, we'd . . ." is another might-have-been that lends a negative air to the meeting. Better to say, "Next meeting we'll plan to discuss . . ." and then be sure it's high on that agenda.

INTRODUCING GUEST SPEAKERS

The best introductions are brief, relate the speaker's competence to the subject he will discuss and suggest how the audience will be able to relate it to their work.

One well-known speaker in the field of fine arts says he's sat on stage and heard his "obituary" read hundreds of times. People charged with introducing him have gone over the details of this man's life to the point that the audience is bored before he begins to speak. What this man decries most is the fact that rarely is mention made of how what he will say relates to the interests of the audience—the very thing he is there to do.

For example, a mortgage banker will address a sales meeting. He recently attended a national convention where new concepts of mortgage lending were discussed and developed. That's the sort of thing to include in the introduction. Skip the facts that he lives on South Boulevard and married Jane Doe 20 years ago.

Help the audience get ready to listen. Listening is awfully hard if you're a salesperson with a lot of pressing problems on your mind and there's no promise of getting help on any of them from this speaker. Maybe you've had trouble putting together a deal on an industrial property because mortgage money has been tight and there's been no indication of a let-up. You'll sit up and listen if the speaker is introduced as a person who has the latest word on the changing money market. Where he got the news and how it is likely to affect your sales in the weeks and months ahead will be of great interest to you.

DON'T GIVE YOUR SPEAKER'S SPEECH

Speakers dread the possibility of being asked to address a group only to have the host make most of their speech for them, even to the point of ascribing opinions to the speaker. Perhaps he does hold a particular opinion; he won't relish having it quoted nakedly or out of context. Let him present his own views in his own way. He may have changed his mind about things since the host last heard him speak. Allow him that freedom. It's not the host's place to say what any speaker "believes."

The opposite extreme is an inadequate introduction. Sometimes no introduction is best of all. A growing number of organizations whose members are told via notices who will be the featured speaker simply have the person come on stage and begin talking. This is certainly to be preferred to an inadequate introduction. Take, for example, the foreman in a western mining camp who is reputed to have introduced an itinerant evangelist: "Here's a feller says his name is Smith. I don't know nothin' about him. He wants to talk to you boys about savin' your souls. You can listen to him if yer a mind to."

That would never happen in a real estate meeting, of course. But speakers tell horror stories about inadequate introductions that convey the impression the host may have heard of the speaker but isn't about to recommend him to the audience. That's hardly the way to capture the attention of the audience and put them in a listening frame of mind. It only reflects a manager's indifference to the value of the time he's invited his salespeople to give to a meeting. Neither they nor the speaker are likely to forget it.

A great deal can be said in very few words. It is well to remember that the first chapter of the Book of Genesis, which covers the creation of "heaven and earth and all that in them is," would require about two 8½ x 11" pages of double spaced typing.

Keep it brief. Give the facts.

INTRODUCING STAFF MEMBERS

Sometimes salespeople are asked to speak at or to conduct an entire meeting. Everybody enjoys an opportunity to stand up and tell how he succeeded.

Introduce that person as one who has had an outstanding month (or a spectacular sale or solved some apparently impossible problem). Don't give his speech for him. Just mention one or two of the highlights from management's point of view (dollar volume, working the area, careful preparation of an involved sale), and stress how anxious people are to learn from successful people, *this* successful person in particular.

Such introductions use a *mutuality of interest* concept, and the salesperson is free to follow in either a *telling* or a *selling* method, or both.

Management's final role in this situation is to end the meeting with a hearty "thank you"—words that every salesperson needs to hear. Selling is a hard business, too seldom rewarded with personal recognition, at least in the eyes of salespeople. Sales meetings provide a fine opportunity to use the pronoun "we" in ways that include everyone, not just top management.

ENDING THE MEETING

Remember the complaint: *"Meetings drag on after the real business has been handled."* A statement in *Alice in Wonderland* contains good advice about when to end a meeting. "Begin at the beginning," the King said gravely, "and go on till you come to the end; then stop."

The pressures of waiting work furnish the best reason in the world for ending a meeting on time or ahead of schedule. If the meeting has been a good one the staff is anxious to get out and start doing some of the things just discussed. Why hold them back just for the sake of using up a predetermined number of minutes? Turn them free. Anyone with something special to discuss will stay anyway.

The late Elmer Wheeler, famed for his sales slogan, "Don't sell the steak, sell the sizzle," had an apt parallel on the importance of a strong finish. It applies to sales meetings as well as selling.

"If," said Wheeler, "you're having a meal in a restaurant, the soup may be cold and the steak tough. But if you can top off with a cup of piping hot, well-brewed coffee, your mood mellows and the tip to the waitress is likely to rise a dime with each succeeding sip."

So it is with meetings. The best ones end in an upbeat fashion with everyone aware that the stated objective can be achieved, anxious to get out and put new ideas to work.

Observe what anchormen on the late evening news practice. The best of the lot end their newscasts with something that gives a lift of spirit. Sometimes it's amusing (though never forced); other times it's a touch of Americana or something to reassure viewers that despite all the cliffhanging news just dispensed we'll all be able to face tomorrow and cope with our problems, finding strength in old and new ways.

Send people forth believing that "getting there is *all* the fun."

INTERVENING WITHOUT MANIPULATING

The manager who encourages each salesperson to give his own unique responses to questions or discussion makes best use of his group. When he understands that each person must be handled with care, even when that person is in the process of putting down another, he is telling the whole group that he respects their egos, which are as tender as his own.

Here are a series of questions or statements that encourage a certain direction without imposing opinions or narrowing concepts. They express an intent but do not restrict thought.[2] With these as a guide, go on to devise more of your own. The questions and statements given here are intended only to suggest how to stimulate thought, encourage individual expression and make salespeople aware of the importance of creative thinking.

OK.
Good, yes?
Do you have an idea how to do that?
What would you like it to be? (*looking for information*)
Great.
How about that? What is your feeling about that?
Any other thoughts about this?
I'd like you to word it . . .
What about that?
What is particularly useful about . . . ?
What is your concern about this?
Can we draw something out of this?
What is appealing about that?
Would you write a goal based on that? (*slight change in subject*)
This is very useful.
I am not sure. Let me hear. (*bring out bashful ideas*)
Let's wish for the real thing.
Good. Great. The more difference the better.
Wait a minute. (*slow speaker down*)
What is your reaction?
Let's put that one down. (*new goal*)
That is the kind of solution I like because . . .
Very interesting.
Say more about it. (*draw out idea*)
Anybody feel different? (*personal analogy*)
What comes to your mind?
I want just anything at all that comes to your mind. (*examine*)
It's fine. (*reassurance*)

Is there some way we could use this so that . . . ? (*overcome objection*)

You have an idea. How might we do that?

Can we improve on this?

Write it down. (*when someone interrupts with new idea*)

How should I word this?

Tell me more.

What do you like about this?

What's on your mind?

Tell us about it—we don't care.

Is there some way we could use this? (*and turn it around*)

Keep talking.

I love the idea that . . . but can we add to that by . . . ?

How can we use this idea?

That's an interesting notion, what do you think?

How about that?

What specifically is implied there that you like? What concerns you about it?

Could you phrase that as a goal?

I'd like you to word it in such a way that it directs us to do something.

What would make this more effective?

Can you give me some words? (*in writing a goal or possible solution*)

I think I've got you. How can we put that? (*discourages person from monopolizing the conversation*)

Can we go on?

Can we do any more with this? If not, shall we make it into a goal?

Anything goes here.

I have the feeling that here is a marvelous goal. If no one has a solution, I'd like to put it up.

How can we turn that into a goal and keep all the pluses?

Rather than raise a philosophical question, can you word it as a goal so we can do something about it?

What are you thinking?

What is your reaction?

Any others?

Have you got it written down?

What is bothering you?

What you said is very desirable.

If I get you what you want to do is . . . (*making sure you understand*)

This notion is very valuable because . . .

Sounds as if it might be a possible solution.
Can you wish for something?
Would you like to address a goal to a bigger problem?
Maybe we can build on that.

MANAGER'S CHECKLIST TO MAKE MOST OF OPPORTUNITIES AT SALES MEETINGS

Make arrangements to prevent interruptions from outside.
Arrive at meeting place a few minutes early.
Confine remarks to subject being discussed.
Listen attentively to all others.
Avoid expressing *absolutes*.
Do not argue.
Keep remarks impersonal.
Be appropriately serious but not solemn.
Respect viewpoints of others.
Avoid long speeches.
When group disagrees, avoid anger or show of annoyance.

---

1. Jay, "How To Run a Meeting," *Harvard Business Review*, March/April 1976.
2. Prince, *The Practice of Creativity*.

CHAPTER 7

Meeting follow-up

Follow-up is the inventory that is taken after the meeting. It is a result of your listening, observing, asking and self-questioning.

KEEP AGENDAS ON FILE

Anything done well is worth using again. Keep your meeting agendas on file both as reminders of what you want to repeat at some future date and as a record of what you've promised to do and/or asked others to do.

A "retired" agenda also will remind you of unexpected things that came up during a meeting—everything from hidden agenda items to an unexpected revolt. Thinking back on this sort of development can help you handle them skillfully in future meetings or perhaps remind you to take action that will avoid future conflict.

LISTENING IS IMPORTANT

Some listening is formal, some casual.

Formal follow-up with staff people starts with one-on-one conversations with those who expressed opposing views or contributed tentative ideas or opinions during the meeting which, for good reason, it was impossible to handle properly at that time. Get back to those people as quickly as possible, bearing in mind the late Walter Lippman's admonition, "Where everyone thinks alike, no one thinks very much."

This can be the most important follow-up to a meeting. As you inquire, probe, question and weigh the salesperson's ideas, contentions or views you are accomplishing two things: first, you are convincing that person that his remarks in the meeting were being listened to and thought worthy of further discussion; second, you are keeping open the upward flow of communication from the staff. This is one of the surest ways to keep future meetings viable.

Casual listening is another matter. It doesn't suggest eavesdropping. Comments made in passing, whether to you directly or between salespeople (but obviously intended for your ears) often provide clues to how the meeting went. If some part of the meeting is discussed with obvious enthusiasm it suggests that the topic or the technique (or both) was successful, could be repeated at future meetings or adapted to other topics. Silence carries the opposite message sometimes, though it could also simply be acceptable and uncontroversial.

OBSERVING THE RESULTS

That 9:05 rule, whereby salespeople put to immediate use what they've learned in a meeting, is one of the best follow-up measures you have. When, for example, the meeting's objective was How To Get More Listings and the office empties out because the staff goes right to work on a new canvassing technique, that spells success. But when the opposite occurs the message is clear to an observant manager that either the staff was playing a Yes role in the meeting or the subject wasn't presented understandably or enthusiastically.

ASKING FOR SUGGESTIONS

A simple form, even the 3 x 5" card that goes in the idea bank, can be offered salespeople with the request that they list topics or techniques they'd like to have included in subsequent meetings. Suggestions may be similar to what's already been done or far off the mark of the firm's tradition. If the suggestions are signed, pursue the suggestion with the person who offered it. (That's continuing upward communication.) If it's not signed, do the best job possible of interpreting what the suggestion implies and get it on a meeting agenda as soon as possible.

SELF-QUESTIONING

The manager's questionnaire at the end of this chapter should produce a fair judgment of how well the meeting went. It will also suggest changes that should be made for the future and how they can be implemented.

QUESTIONNAIRE FOR SALESPEOPLE

Every once in a while ask the staff to participate in a secret ballot about meetings, reacting to their content and telling whether or not they think meetings are necessary. The results may be upsetting but, if so, maybe it's time to shake up the whole process and try to look at it with a pair of fresh eyes.

Here are some of the kinds of questions such a poll might include.

Do you think sales meetings are important? ____Yes ____No
Are they held ____ often enough? ____ too often?
If too often, what schedule do you suggest? _____
Do they last ____ long enough? ____ too long: Comments __
_____

Do they cover topics that concern you? ____Yes ____No
Suggest topics you want included _____
_____

Rate your preference for meeting techniques (1, 2, 3, 4 and 5)
Lecture
Discussion
Role play
Brainstorm
Successful salesperson's report

Would you like more ____information, ____action, ____chance to express opinion? Other comments _____
_____

MANAGEMENT EVALUATION AND HOW TO USE IT

Bill D. Schul, in his book *How To Be an Effective Group Leader*,[1] says a good leader takes inventory often. But just taking inventory isn't enough. It has to be understood and acted upon. A retail merchant, taking semi-annual inventory of his stock, uses it to guide his buying program for the future. He sees what sold well and which merchandise he bought turned out to be "cats and dogs" in the parlance of the trade. He evaluates his inventory and adjusts his buying plan accordingly.

Which parts of a series of sales meetings went well? Which generated greatest participation by most people? What parts of the meetings never seemed to last long enough? What subjects tapered off to a ragged ending with no measurable action taken or recommended? What things were controversial? Should they be explored further? Does the controversy indicate dissatisfaction with the topic at hand or could it be rooted in some other cause?

Reflect on what was good in a meeting, how it could be adapted to future meetings that perhaps have entirely different objectives to achieve. That's creativity combined with good judgment, two traits people expect in their leaders.

Look, too, for needed changes whether in systems, policy or something as simple as discontinuing a required form that is no longer useful. A recent study shows that careful examination of records in one engineering firm reduced 55 forms to 18 because so many of them were kept out of sheer habit! The remaining 18 provide all the information this firm needs for its management control of a business that today is far more sophisticated and more efficient than it was when 55 were kept.

The valid test of the success of every meeting is the action of the people involved after the meeting ends.

AFTER-MEETING CHECKLIST FOR MANAGER

Take a few minutes right after the meeting to follow-up. These 25 questions and their answers can be worth hours of planning time for the next meeting as well as a guide to follow-up with individual salespeople.

	Yes	No
Did meeting start on time?	___	___
Was introduction brief and to the point?	___	___
Was introduction adequate to explain objective of meeting?	___	___
Were salespeople made aware of their role in meeting?	___	___
Was I personally prepared?	___	___
Was I at ease and confident?	___	___
Did I exhibit enthusiasm?	___	___
Did I refrain from lecturing?	___	___
Did I avoid boring repetition of pet phrases?	___	___
Were my statements brief and clear?	___	___
Was my voice clear and well modulated?	___	___
Were my questions well planned and timely?	___	___
Did I use language everyone understood?	___	___
Was I quick to grasp and develop pertinent ideas offered?	___	___
Did I arouse and sustain lively interest?	___	___
Was the objective achieved?	___	___

	Yes	No
Were ideas and situations brought up by salespeople analyzed and clarified?	____	____
Was discussion monopolized by a few?	____	____
Was discussion well distributed?	____	____
Did responses indicate individual thinking?	____	____
Was there a tendency to bickering?	____	____
Did I control that tendency?	____	____
Were there offensive personal comments?	____	____
Was I courteous and tactful?	____	____
Did meeting close on time?	____	____

1. Bill D. Schul, *How To Be an Effective Group Leader.*

In conclusion

Robert Townsend, in *Up the Organization*, says that every success he ever had came about because he was up to his ears helping associates be as effective as possible while having as much fun as possible. In this same context, as your sales meetings help your staff become more effective, your whole operation will be more profitable and more fun for you.

Sales meetings aren't your major business but they are very important to the success of your real estate business.

Remember your people, how important they are to you, how important you are to them. People are always better team players when they are made to feel important to the organization. When you've accomplished this, you're sure to have established good communications, where constructive ideas move in both directions.

What you've read so far in this book will help you develop your own meeting style and your own techniques. The Appendix which follows offers you a rich lode of meeting topics and details on role play, how it works and how to develop a style that best suits you, your people and your situation. The Bibliography suggests periodicals, books and educational courses that will help you make your sales meetings so lively your people will agree that *getting there is all the fun.*

Finally, look at yourself every now and then to see how you're doing. This quiz will help you hold a mirror to what you're doing and how it may look to the people who work with you.

96

Questions to ask yourself at least once every quarter

Am I polishing my image instead of greasing the wheels?

Am I short-tempered with valid criticism?

Do people hesitate before they criticize me?

Am I avoiding risks?

Am I playing it safe?

Am I talking only to certain people?

Do I know my whole sales staff? When did I last talk to them individually?

When did I last try something different?

Which decisions do I make that feed my ego? Which feed the salespeople's egos?

APPENDIX A

Meeting topics

Meeting topics fall into three major categories:

Knowledge
Skills
Attitude.

KNOWLEDGE TOPICS

Knowledge topics cover a broad range, from understanding the local market and the factors and people who influence it, the ethics of the real estate industry and legislation to how a company operates.

SKILLS TOPICS

Skills, the means by which salespeople put knowledge to work, include topics that range from the basics of sales psychology to effective communication with prospects, customers and all the other people needed to be successful in the business. Skills topics also include continuous training and the study of sales techniques proven successful over the years plus new selling concepts as they are developed.

ATTITUDE TOPICS

A healthy attitude toward himself, his fellow workers and the company helps move a salesperson toward success. A good attitude toward oneself and the business can also help salespeople work out of slumps and, in fact, can sometimes prevent a slump from developing. Time management is often a direct reflection of a salesperson's attitude toward his work and himself.

Family relationships can affect a person's attitude toward his work. The hours a real estate salesperson works are not the usual nine-to-five work days of many other people. Living on a commission presents unique problems and opportunities that are easier to handle when understood. They involve the attitude of the salesperson and his family.

TOPICS AFFECT ATTENDANCE

New salespeople come to meetings because they are anxious to learn more about the business. It's not as easy to attract the best people on the staff, the ones who are so busy "making it" they don't want to spend time in a meeting that could be used out on the street working up a transaction. Somewhere between the two extremes are the middle producers, satisfied with the status quo.

Topics have to be found that inform newcomers, challenge the middle group and appeal to the top producers.

"Come tell the bunch how you put that last difficult sale together" can be used with a top producer. Appealing not only to his ego but to the *mutuality of interest* concept, he is less apt to demur at having his secrets "stolen." His presence on the program will bring other top producers interested in knowing what one of the group has accomplished to win management's recognition.

"Come share some of the things you learned about time management at the Marketing Institute course" will be an ego boost to a middle producer who spent his own money for the course and got some ideas he's already put to good use.

"Come share some of the techniques you used in door-to-door selling" can put a new salesperson in front of his peers, able to talk comfortably about a topic with which he is familiar, one that is of concern to all of them.

Topics that appeal to the team spirit are more likely to result in good, action-packed meetings.

Topic possibilities are virtually limitless. So, too, are the ways the whole staff can participate. When people are encouraged to participate and are assured the meeting will hold a tangible benefit for them, the problem of low attendance dwindles.

HOW QUICKLY DO PEOPLE ABSORB INFORMATION?

Some people grasp ideas quickly from conversation; others respond better to written material. The first reactions of some people are best; later on they're not so sure. Others can't be rushed, need to "sleep on it."

Topics can be chosen to provide useful information and stimulation to both kinds of people. Repeating a subject at a later meeting often brings reactions and convictions from the kind of people who need to think a thing through on their own.

Another value in repeating a topic is that it gives a chance to ask one or two who show enthusiasm for an idea the first time around to come back in a week and report to the group whether or not they think the idea makes sense. That gives a pretty good idea whether the sales staff is going to adopt the idea and try to make it work or whether the other extreme is the case and an apology should be offered the group for wasting their time.

AIM FOR BALANCE BETWEEN STABILITY AND CHANGE

Plan a series of meetings to cover topics that relate to each other, so there is some continuity from one meeting to the next. Each might review the elements of a technique or skill that remains unchanged; then devote some discussion or perhaps a brainstorming session to developing new techniques. Such a series might include listing techniques, qualifying the buyer, showing the property, and negotiating or presenting the offer to the seller.

TOPICS MAY BE ACADEMIC OR PRACTICAL

Topics used in an academic way set up a hypothetical situation, then seek a possible solution. Practical problems, on the other hand, reflect actual situations encountered by the staff. When they have been handled successfully, the staff person is asked to tell the group what the problem was and how it was handled. When salespeople fail they can often be persuaded to share their frustrations with their peers and ask or suggest themselves how things could have been done differently.

MEETING TOPICS THAT AREN'T

Frustration or anger sometimes leads to spending valuable meeting time on subjects that alienate sales associates. Resist the urge to "tell 'em off." The ones who deserve it are most likely absent and those present resent wasting their time listening to lectures about the shortcomings of others.

For example, take the manager who, frustrated by low attendance week after week, devoted an entire staff meeting to a lecture on absenteeism. He alienated those present who had come to learn something, not to listen to a sermon on shortcomings of others. The absentees later suffered the antagonism of those who had listened to the tirade.

If, instead of a harsh lecture, salespeople at that meeting had been given some sure-fire knowledge they could use that week, word would have gotten around and chances are good that meeting attendance would have improved the next week.

Another example of an unsuitable topic is the manger who spent an entire meeting going over the monthly phone bill, item by item, demanding to know who'd made each toll call, to whom and for what purpose. That manager would have been better off checking with the phone company for suggestions on better record keeping, then quietly instituting needed changes. He could then use a sales meeting to do something positive about phone costs, saying "the high phone bill is preventing our doing some things we all consider important. If we can control phone costs, for example, we can use the dollars saved to get that company brochure we all want. Here are some ways we can all work together to control our phone costs. . . ."

Or the same meeting would have been better had time been given to reviewing telephone *skills*, brainstorming when to make long distance calls or exploring other means of communication that might work as well at lower cost.

"Praise in public, punish in private" is a good rule of thumb in deciding what things properly deserve meeting time and what needs to be dealt with in a one-to-one situation with individuals.

REPEATING TOPICS

When it is necessary to repeat a topic again and again, make it new. Paraphrasing Gilbert Highet's words in *The Immortal Profession*, there is a need for renewal in everyone. Approach the topic from a fresh point of view. Invite a visitor to talk on the subject. When a good new book on the topic comes out, digest it and discuss it in a meeting. If possible, have at least one or two others read it in advance and come prepared to offer their comments. When topics that need repeating are handled in this way, you are not repeating. You are reinforcing creatively. Keeping all agendas will remind you what worked well in past meetings and will remind you to repeat the best topics.

THERE ARE NO PERMANENT SOLUTIONS

The game of golf has been described as a succession of bad habits. The player works to correct a slice only to have his iron shots go to pot. Practice corrects that and suddenly putting deteriorates. So it is with managing a sales staff. Meetings offer weekly opportunities for correcting bad practices in selling but promise no permanent cures. It's simply a matter of trying over and over again to correct bad practices, assume a better stance and keep up a dogged determination that the next "game" will go a little better.

You have to go after problems again and again, attacking them in different ways—role play, discussion, etc. The principles are repeated but with a change in the script.

Here are some of the limitless topics you can use as the base of your meeting objective. Separated by knowledge, skills and attitude, you will find many of them repeated under each heading. The repetition is intentional, for many topics apply to all three areas in the field of real estate sales.

Go beyond these suggestions and add your own ideas, writing them down when they occur to you. You may not be able to use them this week, but when they're written they'll be there for future use.

KNOWLEDGE TOPICS
Company operation

Company history and philosophy
Policy and procedures—avoid spending time on minutiae
Ethics
Consumerism—warranties and how they work
    —fraud and malpractice
Budget and planning as they affect salespeople
Advertising—what is used and why
    —what it does for company and salespeople
    —how its effectiveness is measured
Public relations—everybody every day
Working conditions—floor time, hours, weekends
    —how it works for both the staff and the company
Forms—use of and benefits

Marketing area

Definition of the "real estate market"
Unique characteristics of this market. Are they changing? How?
Supply and demand
Business cycles
Business—manufacturing, industrial, retail, services

Employment opportunities
Education facilities
Health care facilities
Religious organizations
Recreation and sports facilities—public and private
Cultural opportunities—music, art, drama, study groups,
   libraries

Market conditions

The pulse of this market
Too many listings—how to handle and keep sellers satisfied
Too few listings
Sales too slow
Sales too fast—customers complain "no time to think things
   over"
What is selling and why
Future projections—new industries, new residential develop-
   ments
      —where should company be a year from now? How to get
         there?
Ten minutes for tipsters—properties coming on the market,
   price changes, seller motive changes

Marketing methods, techniques and aids

Appraising
REALTOR® Code of Ethics
Competitive market analysis
Depreciation
Exchanging
Financing
   Conventional financing
   Money supply—when it's plentiful
      —when it's scarce—27 ways to finance in a tight market
      —private investors, how to find
   FHA-VA mortgages
   Other government-insured finance
   Purchase money loans
   Usury laws
Income property analysis
Land values projecting
Legislation (as it affects marketing)
   Local, state, national
   What we win, what we lose and why
   How salespeople can help influence it—REALTORS® Poli-
      tical Action Committee

Product

Houses
Land
Apartments
Condominiums
Cooperatives
Commercial
Industrial

Real estate math

Using hand calculator
Ellwood tables

Real estate vocabulary
Sale-leasebacks
Subleases

Taxation
Municipal
County
State
National

Professional growth

Study courses—local Board, Marketing Institute, other
Meetings—local Board, State Association, National Association
Reading—business and professional publications
Organization dues—what they're used for, value of membership
Trends in industry—what they are
    —what they mean
    —how to explain them to the public
Civic and community involvement

SKILLS TOPICS

Communications

How to handle telephone inquiries on sign call-ins
How to handle telephone inquires on ads
How to talk—prospecting, qualifying, showing, negotiating, closing
How to listen—prospecting, qualifying, showing, negotiating, closing
How to use the telephone (phone company speaker or film)

Making personal calls count—how to distribute more business cards

Communicating with the boss

Developing transactions

Brochures and leaflets that help

Closing techniques

Emotion vs. logic

Extra services

Follow-up techniques

Group selling—when it pays, how it works

Ideas that click

Importance of impressions

Importance of listening and looking

Preparing the presentation

Salesmanship in a presentation

Secrets of creativity

Servicing listings

Using other sales techniques in real estate

Wrong ways to sell

Development and improvement of techniques

Biggest competitor—For Sale by Owner—new ways to approach and sell

Company services and how to sell them

Follow-ups on both buyers and sellers

Handling a settlement

How to convince sellers of For Sale sign benefits

How to deal with an unhappy buyer

How to stimulate intra-office cooperation

How to stimulate inter-office cooperation

How to sustain drive in slow markets

Listings—how to sell them creatively

Problem properties—brainstorm solutions

Using slow periods to reformulate good habits

Personal and professional development

Attaining professional status

Been to a course? Share highlights with staff

Characteristics of a successful salesperson

Civic and community involvement

Company library—what's available and how to use it

Developing centers of influence

Goals

Habits
How to plan your work
How your family can help
Improving your self image
Know your business
Letter writing
Needs—Maslow's hierarchy
Prestige—the company's and yours
Professional meetings
Professional organizations—costs
        —value of membership
Promote yourself in business community
Public speaking
Reading—business and professional
Slumps—how to avoid
        —how to work out of
Study courses—local, Marketing Institute, others
Values of good reputation

Retraining

Closings—how to proceed
        —how to "recognize the moment"
Developing a farm—how to specialize in a defined area
        —ten ways to set up a farm where canvassing prohibited
How to anticipate a selling season
How to anticipate a listing season
Handling objections
How to find listings
How to find prospects
How to discuss government regulations with customers
How to use company p.r. materials in presentations
How varying interest rates, used properly, permit financing
Making a listing presentation
Negotiating price with buyer
Negotiating price with seller
Understanding warranties
Ten new ideas to use on any of the above

Sales psychology

Understanding sellers and buyers
   Reasons for selling—what they say, what they mean
   Reasons for buying—what they say, what they mean
How one salesperson handled a particularly difficult listing
How one salesperson handled a particularly difficult sale
How to make every call count

How to promote yourself in the business community
How the company prestige can help you make sales

ATTITUDE TOPICS

Company loyalty
Compliance with policy and procedures
   Daily hours, floor time, weekend hours
   Records—why needed, how used
Cooperating with competitors
   Legal obligation to sellers
   Moral obligaton to buyers
Daily dress—why appearance matters
Living on a commission income
Maslow's hierarchy of needs
Personal drive—in a fast market
   —in a slow market
REALTOR® Code of Ethics
Sales meetings—punctuality and participation
Self-motivation—the only kind
Time management—what others do
   —how to develop your own
Working with office staff
Working with other salespeople

OUTSIDE SPEAKERS

Outside speakers need basic information about who they will be talking to and why. Most will ask essential questions about how they can relate their expertise to the needs of your group. Tell them the kind of information and guidance they can supply, whether to focus on knowledge, skills or attitude, the time limits for their remarks, whether or not they will be asked questions (and be sure they agree to answer them). Confirm in writing when and where the meeting will be held.

Business

Chamber of Commerce manager—local business/sales data and predictions
Management people from local industries—explain their operation and future plans that may affect your firm's plans; both residential and industrial employment opportunities in their operation
Sales reps—termite damage to properties
   —burglar alarm systems
   —any business your firm should know more about
   —how other salespeople sell their products or services

Insurance broker—the vocabulary of insurance in real estate
and homeowners policies

Telephone company rep—how to use phone professionally
—market data from the local phone company
—future of the telephone in the real estate business

Educators

Athletic coach—team spirit and how it works for everyone
—importance of continued training

English instructor—how to write letters
—speed reading and how to make it work for you

Psychologists—sales psychology
—understanding Maslow's hierarchy of needs

Marketing instructor—how to study and understand markets
—how to use what you learn
—repeat business sources

Economics instructor—what to read to keep abreast of the
business market
—how to interpret what you read and apply it to real
estate

Librarian—local business, public and university libraries and
how to use them
—how to build your personal business library

Finance

Banker—money market, present and future outlook, seasonal
money patterns

Savings and loan officer—money supply, legislation, FHA,
VA, GNMA and others

Government

Recorder from County Court House—records, why and how
they are kept
—how to make your work and his easier

Zoning commissioner—new ordinances

City planner

Services commissioners—streets, sanitation, water

Tax assessor—how properties measured, when
—how appeal assessments and taxes

Agency officials—schools, library, parks, public health services, hospitals to explain their agency, its functions and
services

Local officials—building codes, planning, public services,
finance, taxes
—how citizens and business community should participate
and why

Other sales fields

Insurance—how life insurance recruits for prospects; timing skills; closes sales

Door to door salespeople or supervisors—Avon, Fuller brush
—how they operate, secrets of their success, their follow-up techniques and timing

Associate from competing firm—how he works with FSBO prospects
—how he develops a territory

Services and professions related to real estate

Ad agency rep—how to write copy, how to work with media people

Appraiser—how he judges market value, measures he uses

Architect—building styles, restrictions, lot lines, zoning, building materials, renovating, converting, restoring old structures

Contractor/builder—construction techniques, costs, materials

Executive officer of local Board

Communications people—newspaper, radio, TV
—how to prepare copy for them
—how to convey business news they can use in form they need
—interview shows—how they work, how to get on them

Lawyer—situations encountered at closing, escrow, title variations

Real estate commissioner—what he does, how he does it, why
—license laws

Taxes

IRS agent—real estate rulings
—personal income tax problems of salespeople—how to save on taxes

CPA—Accounting principles for business and personal records
—Investing commission income
—How to keep good tax records

OTHER SOURCES OF MEETING MATERIALS

Where can you turn for help in finding meeting topics and materials that will make the sessions appealing and useful to your salespeople?

Daily reading is invaluable. It can be as diverse as the *Wall Street Journal,* business sections of daily newspapers and weekly magazines and special real estate publications such as *real estate today®*, devoted to serving you. Your local board, regional groups, state and the NATIONAL ASSOCIATION OF REALTORS® also supply members with regular publications and occasionally special journals.

The finest real estate library outside the Library of Congress is the Herbert U. Nelson Library of the National Association. It services thousands of requests from individual REALTORS® every year, sending books and other materials out of loan to members. A request addressed to the librarian will bring you a brochure explaining the service and how you can use it.

Your public library and many business college and university libraries are also good sources of print and, occasionally, audio/visual materials which you may borrow. And if your public library is a member of a library "system" it may be the repository of business titles for the system; it will surely have access to those materials on inter-library loan.

The fact that you have this book indicates that you know about Marketing Institute publications. Keep up to date on what's in the catalog so you can add new titles to your business library as they are published.

APPENDIX B

Role play

REAL ESTATE MANAGERS ROLE PLAY ALMOST EVERY DAY

You role play as you counsel salespeople who are in a slump. You role play with successful salespeople who have stopped doing the very things that made them so successful, whether telephone techniques, prospecting or whatever. You role play most of all with new salespeople who need help every day on how to handle situations they've not faced before.

Little wonder then that role play is so popular in sales meetings. Everyone who has participated in it to some degree knows it's the best and surest way to prepare for what they are likely to encounter and that it is done at a minimum of cost—only their meeting time. Listings and sales are never lost in role play but, when well done, the training it gives can prevent actual dollar loss, damaged egos and jeopardized relationships with clients in the real world of selling.

When salespeople learn to do their thinking in advance, in a sense preparing for emergencies before they happen, they gain poise. But if they come upon a situation unprepared, they lack the self assurance needed to handle things well. Role playing not

111

only teaches actual techniques in real estate, but it trains people to take time to collect their thoughts and to think through a situation "on their feet."

DO IT YOUR WAY

Regardless of the situation to be played, a specific environment or scene should be set. The tone should be kept positive and the atmosphere as relaxed as possible. You have to be comfortable if your people are to be relaxed about this technique. Examine the various ways role play is used by REALTORS® and choose the one with which you will be most comfortable. Do it your way. Take the basic rules, use the techniques you think will work best for you and your people and you'll have a popular addition to lively sales meetings.

Rules of the game

No matter what technique you follow (and there are many good ones) certain general rules apply to every role play situation.

State the situation.
Allow participants time to prepare.
Set the stage.
Do not interrupt during the play.
End it when a good point has been made or when "time" is up.
Critique on the positive side.

State the situation

The situation can be stated to both parties, or only one side of it to each party. If a role play is spontaneous, as in a break during a film or tape cassette, the play situation will have been set up in the audio/visual and you will simply assign roles to selected people.

Allow participants time to prepare

Some role play situations may need only a couple minutes to prepare, others may be assigned as much as a week or a day in advance of your meeting. In the case of audio/visual breaks, of course, no time for preparation is given because it will be wholly spontaneous. Variety adds spice to the game.

Set the stage

The typescript will set the stage. In some cases considerable detail is given, in others only the barest facts. Sometimes the desired result will be stated; in other cases, REALTORS® like to give that responsibility to the role players.

Do not interrupt

Interruptions break the pace of role play and inhibit the participants. No matter how far the play may get from what you had in mind, don't interrupt.

Critique on the positive side

The participants are the first to participate in the critique. Five questions will help them review what they've just done.

Are you satisfied with your control of the situation?
Did the other party surprise you with any responses or attitudes?
If you could do it over, would you change any of your lines?
Would you now feel more confident in a similar, real life situation?
Would you like to do it again at another meeting?

Next, the audience critiques. It is important to establish beforehand that *all* comments are to be on the positive side.

What did the salesperson do right?
What were his strongest responses?
If you'd been in his place, what would you have done differently?
Would you like to participate in role play at another meeting?

IMPORTANT POINTS TO REMEMBER

Realism is essential. Both the situation and the characters must be true to life. A positive approach is required. People are there to learn what *will* work. It's a waste of time to focus on what won't succeed. It should be serious. There is no place for jokes or funny asides. Silence is essential. There should be no kibitzing, even from you. There is a set time limit, usually five minutes from the time play begins. There are no "second chances" in a single play. It may be replayed, but there is no backing up with "I should have said . . ." Neither salesperson nor client nor manager deviates from the role as assigned.

THE VARIABLES

Some managers believe in handing out single scripts, where each person knows only his situation. The salesperson has only the details of his role, the one playing the customer role has only his. Some managers give full details to both or, in the case of more than two, all the people involved in the play. Still other managers always play the role of the customer because it is their belief that role play is used to develop responses and it is confusing when salespeople are asked to think themselves into the role of the customer. The reverse side of this, of course, is the strong feeling of other managers that their salespeople need to role play as customers so they'll be more alert to what their real-life customers may be thinking, saying, or not saying.

Here again, examine the various techniques and choose the one you believe will work best for you and your people. Only you know their needs and how you can help fill them.

If you know your people well enough and believe they need to be "loosened up" for role play, you may use touches of humor in the briefing stage. For example, in setting up a particularly diffi-cult problem, you may ask a salesperson to "come right over here and stand over the trap door," or "to play this one, Mary, get as close to the ground as you can. This customer's really got it in for you!" If you use humor this way, be sure to establish the rule that it isn't to be carried over into the role play itself.

Some managers even rehearse role plays the first time around with new salespeople, realizing that the participants will be more relaxed if they know a little bit about what to expect. These managers claim that rehearsal doesn't destroy the spon-taneity of what follows.

WHEN SALESPEOPLE PLAY BOTH ROLES

Each is handed a sheet of paper detailing the situation. It may provide only one role or it may include both. Many real life situations will reflect full knowledge or very limited information, so either technique is valuable. Some role plays give a great deal of background information, others very little. The following pages provide samples of role play that involve salespeople play-ing both roles.

All these role plays are used by REALTORS® who find them useful in generating enthusiastic participation by salespeople.

OVERCOMING A SELLER'S OBJECTIONS

Seller's Role

Your name is Mr. Smart and you have been transferred to Cali-fornia. You've been trying to sell your three-bedroom ranch by yourself for the last few weeks, and you have just about given up. About the only calls you have been receiving are from those darn real estate salespeople; in fact, you have finally decided to let a few of them come over so that you can get their opinions about your house.

Right now Jim Sellrite, a salesperson from A B C, REALTORS®, is in your living room and he seems pretty turned on about the house. He suggests a $48,500 sales price and $49,900 list price. That seems pretty good to you. That's right in line with what your bowling buddy Mark Lucky told you.

Actually it's a good thing Mrs. Smart is shopping for the evening. She usually confuses important matters such as this, and you feel that, when this fellow Sellrite leaves, you should call your bowling buddy. Although you only see him three hours a week those ten bowling weeks a year, he is not a bad guy and his feelings would probably be hurt if you didn't list with him. So you say to Jim Sellrite, "Well, I've got this friend of mine that works for X Y Z Realty who I think I'll list with."

Salesperson's role

Your name is Jim Sellrite and you've been a salesperson for A B C, REALTORS® for about three months. The company has had a big push to obtain exclusive listings since they are extremely tight, and you've been spending the bulk of your time in the last few weeks chasing down "By Owner" ads. So far you've had absolutely no luck, and this is pretty aggravating because not only have you spent time, but other salespeople in your office seem to be bringing in some listings, and you sure don't want to be the one without any.

You thought you would try another "By Owner" ad, and you find that Mr. Smart, who is being transferred to San Francisco, has just about given up trying to sell his home himself. (Mrs. Smart is out shopping for the evening, but it seems Mr. Smart makes the decisions anyway.) You were able to get an appointment and you gave him your estimated selling price of $48,500 and suggested listing price of $49,900. He quite agreed. Hey, it looks like you finally struck gold!

But now as you are sitting right in his living room, he looks you squarely in the face and says that he is thinking of listing with Mark Lucky, who works for X Y Z Realty, since Mark has been on his bowling team for about three years.

PROSPECTING

REALTOR®-ASSOCIATE—Housewife (two people for role play)

Situation

Salesperson learns from neighbor that prospective sellers are being transferred. This is the first contact made. Housewife's initial response is that they thought they would only consider listing their home with the salesperson that sold it to them.

What approach should a salesperson use to overcome this objection and secure an appointment for an inspection?

PROSPECTING

REALTOR® -ASSOCIATE—Prospective Buyer (two people for role play)

Situation

You are on the floor and a phone call comes in on one of your ads. The buyer wants all the information about the home including the address. Your job is to give him just enough information that will make him interested in the property and also make it possible for you to make an appointment. How do you handle a call-in like this?

QUALIFYING

REALTOR® -ASSOCIATE—Mr. and Mrs. Buyer (three people for role play)

Situation

The customers walk into your office on your floor time. Having never met them before, you know nothing about their needs as to size of home, location, possession, price, or amount of money they wish to invest in a home. To give your customers the best service possible and at the same time not be overly aggressive, what approach should you use in qualifying a buyer such as this?

NEGOTIATING THE CONTRACT (SELLERS)

REALTOR® -ASSOCIATE—Mr. and Mrs. Seller (three people for role play)

Situation

Your sale—A B C listing at $55,900. You have asked your buyer to come in with his best offer. He signs the contract for $54,500 which you believe is a good offer. Home has been on the market just three days. Because it is a new listing, the seller will not accept contract only because of price and wants to counter at $55,500. What is the best approach to negotiate this contract?

GETTING THE LISTING

Situation

Mr. and Mrs. Young have owned their home three years; purchased on FHA-VA low equity; placed FSBO ad in Sunday paper.

Scene

Owner's home
Monday 2 P.M.
Sales Associate rings door bell
Mrs. Young answers door.
Sales Associate: "Good afternoon, Mrs. Young, I'm _____
    from _____ REALTORS®

Mrs. Young knows

Mr. Young's job promotion requires private home office for research and reports. They have moved three children into one
bedroom now to give him office space. The new job requires
some overnight travel so a second car must now be purchased;
salary increase not great enough to allow car purchase and
higher monthly house payments, but if they can sell the present
home at highest price possible without expenses of REAL-
TOR®'S commission, they might find larger home they could
manage.

Mrs. Young's goal

Sell without REALTOR®.

Sales associate knows

Market has appreciated approximately 11 percent since the
Youngs purchased three years ago. Several new developments
offer similar homes with builder's assistance in financing arrangements and builders paying buyer's closing costs.

Sales associate's goal

Secure appointment to meet with Mr. and Mrs. Young to present
market value analysis on property.

AVOIDING CANCELLATION

Situation

Property has been on the market 60 days of 120 day listing.
Priced 10 percent above market value analysis recommenda-
tion. Few showings, no offers. Mr. Owner started new job in
another city 30 days ago, now home only every other weekend.
New job city more expensive real estate market. Another REAL-
TOR® listed and sold neighboring house last week.

Scene

REALTOR®'S office Saturday A.M.
Mr. Owner: "I've got to sell this house of ours and you obviously
can't do it, so I want to list it with X. They really get the job done!"

Mr. Owner knows

Mrs. Owner is threatening divorce if the family doesn't get settled soon; too much responsibility for her.

Mr. Owner's goal

Cancel this listing!

Sales associate knows

Competitor's fast sale was 5 percent below opinion of market value. Prospects not interested in looking at listed price, with others to select.

Sales associate's goal

Get price reduced and retain the listing!

THE EMPTY HOUSE

Situation

Suburban home vacant. Owner lives in city. Has FSBO sign advising "key next door" and listing owner's phone. Neighbor has told sales associate that Mr. Owner has offered $100 for his services if he shows property to a buyer.

Scene

REALTOR®'S office
Mr. Owner brings information sheet into office and offers to pay 3 percent commission is sold.

Mr. Owner knows

Legal fees of probate will probably leave no funds from father's small estate. The empty house probably his only chance to pocket any money, if he can sell it quickly with least expense possible. Believes "opening door" for prospects can bring about a sale, or all REALTOR® firms will be glad to bring their prospects and he could pay 3 percent for that if they sell it for 3 percent more than he will sell it through the neighbor's kind services.

Mr. Owner's goal

Enlist aid of all REALTORS® in selling on open listing.

Associate knows

Broker will not approve any associate working with open listings with no commission protection on their prospects.

Associate's goal

Secure exclusive right to sell listing.

THE EXPIRED LISTING
Situation
Property listed for 90 days.
Priced 10 percent above market value.
Few showings. No offers.
Listing associate has not communicated with owner for past 30 days.
Listing expired yesterday.
FSBO sign in yard today.

Scene
Owner's front door.
Sales associate rings doorbell.
Mr. Owner: "You're too late now! I've had this listed with one of you REALTORS® for three months. Where were you when you had the chance to sell it then? Now I'm going to sell it myself!"

Mr. Owner knows
He can't depend on any REALTORS®. List your house and you never hear from them again! Neighbor told him he got his price when he sold his house last month, and this house is nicer than the neighbor's.

Mr. Owner's goal
Get rid of all REALTORS®!

Sales associate knows
No property in this neighborhood has sold for past 30 days because of pending zoning hearing to make one side of block commercial. Last sale of neighboring house was by investor who has applied for the zoning change and plans to put service station on the corner, after removing the house he purchased.

Sales associate's goal
Secure opportunity to prepare market value analysis based on pending zoning change, determine urgency for sale, and secure owner's trust.

"RENTERS"
Situation
Mr. and Mrs. Transferee have arrived from another state and want to "rent awhile" until they know the area, since they have 18 months before they have to reinvest profits from sale of former home.

Scene

REALTOR®'S office
Mr. and Mrs. Transferee come in to ask about rentals.

Mr. and Mrs. Transferee know

They made a mistake in judgment on purchase of former home bought in the wrong neighborhood and realized loss when resold.

Mr. and Mrs. Transferee's goal

Caution! Don't buy anything till you know for sure about neighborhood and property values in area.

Sales associate knows

Rentals are scarce in the community. This is suburban residential area with no "undesirable" locations, simply preference of proximity to schools, shopping, transportation, and price range.

Sales associate's goal

Secure appointment to "sell the community" and then look for a house to buy!

SECURE THE LISTING!

Situation

Owner has permitted sales associate to prepare market value analysis and is now listening to listing presentation.

Owner

"Well, we do have several people who are interested in the property and guess we should give them time to make up their minds, since we can sell it to them cheaper."

Goal

Secure the listing!

PRICE OBJECTIONS

Situation

Sales associate has prepared market value analysis on property and is in owner's home making listing presentation.

Owner

"But we think our home should sell for more than that . . ."

Goal

Secure listing at not more than 5 percent above market value recommendation.

FULL SERVICE—FULL COMMISSION

Situation

FSBO property sign has been removed, after being on lawn for two weeks. Owners have decided they need professional help.

Sales associate

Knocks on door to inquire if property has "sold." Learning it has not but is still "for sale," seeks to have opportunity to prepare market value analysis and make listing presentation.

Owner

"How much commission do you charge?"

Sales associate

"On your property, we would act as your agents for 6 percent commission on the sale."

Owner

"Why should I let you list it then, when X Y Z will list for only 4 percent?"

Goal

Convince "full service earns full commission."

"WE HAVE A FRIEND . . ."

Situation

Newspaper item has just revealed promotion—transfer of owners of home in prime neighborhood. Sales associate calls to congratulate owner and secure information about relocation plans, and appointment to talk about listing the local property.

Owner's response and attitude

"We have a friend who has a real estate license."

Goal

Secure appointment for professional market value analysis and referral to new location.

WHEN THE MANAGER PLAYS THE CUSTOMER'S ROLE FIRST

The manager sets the tone of the situation and sees that it's done right. This method, by example, shows salespeople that no one should set out to "beat" another by doing things that do not occur in real life situations, the kind of inside information and arguments that are not a legitimate part of role play.

Later, the customer's role is assigned to salespeople who the manager knows to be relaxed and self-assured enough to handle it well, or to someone who needs recognition, perhaps a senior staffer or a top salesperson. When this is done, the manager sets it up with these people in advance but handles it in the meeting as a spontaneous situation.

Here are several role plays used in this fashion.

Situation

Scene

Owner's home. Listing is 60 days old. Salesperson has been told to get the price down to the market.

Facts

Two showings, eight ads, no offers. Listed $4,000 over market for 120 days.

Customer's outlook

Mr. and Mrs. Seller's new home is under roof. Salesperson has not been in touch. Doors of present house left unlocked—lights on. Nearby home sold by competitor recently. Salesperson went to high school with Mrs. Owner. Husband opens with: "Well stranger—got our place sold yet?"

Situation

Scene

REALTOR®'S Office 9:00 P.M.
Second showing is over. All went well.

Facts

Property on the market four days—eight showings, priced right, good strong motive for selling.

Customer's outlook

Mr. and Mrs. "Never-Pay-Retail" have looked for six months. Now rent month to month. No money problem—but no decision either. Wife opens with: "We sure like that house but we think it's much more than we want to pay. We're really in no hurry, you know."

Situation

Scene

Office of owner who had salesperson check a two-family invest-ment property for him. He inherited it and now wants to sell it. It's a nice $26,000, 20-year old place—needs work.

Customer's outlook

Mr. Owner opens with: "You come recommended—that's why I called you. Now, I'll list with you for 30 days at $34,500. Do a good job and I'll extend it for another 30, and I don't want any sign or nosey neighbors and the price is firm—I got an appraisal. (Discovers 7 percent commission on contract.)

WHEN THE MANAGER PLAYS THE CUSTOMER'S ROLE

Some managers feel role play works best if they assume the role of the customer, emphasizing the importance of the salesperson developing his selling skills rather than focusing on customer roles.

One manager calls in from five to eight salespeople who are low producers. He has role play situations typed on 3 x 5" cards, shuffles them and asks a salesperson to take one. The sales-person is given a few minutes to read the situation and think about it. The salesperson then reads the card to the group and he and the manager role play it. In this office, a commercial-invest-ment firm, the critique is offered by the rest of the group.

Role play can be as creative as the manager who directs it, as you can see from some of this office's commercial-investment role plays.

A property owner has come into your office to visit you and list his property with you. After giving you complete details, when he tells you the price, it is obvious to you that it is about 50 percent too much. What do you say?

You have submitted a contract to a land owner. The contract seems to be acceptable, except for the terms which are five years interest only and a ten–year payout. The property owner does not seem to understand "interest only," or mortgages. This is the only real estate transaction in which he has ever been involved.

A man is interested in relocating his business and seems to like an industrial building which you have shown him. As far as you can tell, everything fits his requirements. You have just completed inspecting the property and are standing in the reception area of the building.

You have made a "cold" call on a property owner trying to get a listing on property he owns. He makes this statement: "No, I'm not interested in selling that property, but I surely am interested in making a good real estate investment."

You have just shown a business lot to a possible user which seemed to fit all of his requirements. He tells you he thinks the lot is too narrow, that the traffic isn't heavy enough, and he's afraid that it's filled with stuff that will make his building settle.

Your prospect has made an offer on one of your listings and the offer was satisfactory in every way except price. The owner turned down the offer and refused to make a counteroffer. You are trying to get your prospect to raise his offer so that you can go back another time.

You have a prospect for a certain piece of property. When you call on the owner he informs you that his price is $100,000 net and he doesn't want to be obligated to pay any commission under any circumstances.

A property owner is very interested in having you work on his property, and you think that you can sell it. However, it is a very complex property and will require a lot of research and preparation. It is obvious that you will need an exclusive. The property owner agrees to a 15-day exclusive listing.

You have shown income property to an investor who is willing and able to buy it. He has inspected the property with you. You have supplied him with all the details. He seems to be interested in the property. Three days after inspecting the property you are seated in the investor's office and he says, "Let me think about it a little while."

You have just met a gentleman at a party and when he hears that you're in the real estate business he comments that he is thinking about looking for a new location for his business.

Three months have expired on your six month exclusive listing. You have worked hard on the property but have no active prospects at this time. You thought the price was right when you accepted the listing but now you are convinced that it is over-priced. You are meeting with the owner in his office to discuss a price reduction for the duration of the exclusive.

You have just finished walking over a 20-acre condominium site with a potential developer and have returned to your car.

You have spotted an owner's "for sale" sign on a piece of property that looks interesting to you. You've looked up the owner and have called on him at his place of business and found him in and able to see you. What do you say?

You are making a cold call on the regional manager of a national concern whose responsibility is the operation of a 20,000-square-foot warehouse.

TAPING THE SESSIONS

If you have audio or video taping equipment, use it to record role plays. An immediate playback following the critique will reveal to the participants what they sounded and/or looked like, even to the length of their pauses for thinking things through. It's all grist for the mill in developing skills in selling. The more it is used the more comfortable people will feel about having their words and expressions recorded.

In a training situation, role play is handled in greater depth and for a longer period. The time limits of a sales meeting limit role play to perhaps 15 minutes with a single, short-term goal. Five minutes are used in actual role play, ten minutes to critique it. If a manager wants everybody to participate he can break the group into teams.

PROBLEMS AND HOW TO COPE WITH THEM

Some salespeople will be really up against it, at first unable to express themselves. When a manager knows his people well, he'll know how a single word can move such a person off dead center. But he's careful not to intrude beyond a word or two because that takes the situation out of the salesperson's hands.

In most groups someone is an absolute ham. Then the manager nudges the role play along with a one-liner like "you've got 30 seconds to get them to sign that purchase." It's said in a way that stresses the value of time, never to get a laugh.

ROLE PLAY BECOMES POPULAR

Many managers, reluctant to introduce role play at first, report
that after watching a series over several meetings they find their
own enthusiasm growing and the staff asking for more chances
to use it.

MASS ROLE PLAY

Take a meeting with ten people. Keep five in the room, send five
into the hall. Give the first five the situation: "You're customers,
being transferred into town. Your teen-age daughter doesn't
want to come."

Now call in the other five. Tell them: "You're going to be
talking to these potential buyers. They are transferees who
called and made this appointment. You're seeing them in your
office. Find out what their problem is."

Pair them off, one from each group against another.

The role play is all done in front of the group, two by two.
Nothing is in writing. It all relies on how they ask their questions
and whether they use the company form for qualifying.

ON-SITE ROLE PLAY

This very realistic role play takes place in a listing that's vacant.
Ask participants to demonstrate how to show a home. One sales-
person plays his own role, two others the parts of Mr. and Mrs.
Homebuyer.

Critique on the site.

SOME OTHER SUGGESTED ROLE PLAYS

How to qualify buyer—money, ticklish questions, errors
made, lost prospects
Showing properties—approaching property, talking in car,
psyching prospect for property to be shown
Leading buyer to make little decisions as you move to big
decision—to buy
Negotiating price with sellers—dozen or more ways
Cross-showings—when two salespeople from two different
firms arrive to show a property at the same time
Telephone calls inquiring price or location of classified ad
Cold canvassing
Farms
For Sale by Owners
How to get in the door
How to present offer to sellers
How to give out more business cards—what to use as reason
for dropping in on people with "useful" information, and
what is "useful" information and how it can be followed up.

Bibliography

Barry, Maude. *Managing Meetings.* New York: John Wiley & Sons, Inc., 1975.

Batten, J. D. *Tough-Minded Management.* New York: American Management Association, 1963.

Berne, Eric, M. D. *What Do You Say After You Say Hello?* New York: Grove Press, Inc., 1972.

_____ Games People Play, 1967.

Brainstorms for Salespeople. REALTORS® NATIONAL MARKETING INSTITUTE, 1976.

"Brainstorms: The 100 Percent Concept." *real estate today®* , May/June 1976.

Clark, Charles H. *Brainstorming.* Garden City, NY: Doubleday, 1958.

Drucker, Peter F. *Management: Tasks, Responsibilities, Practices.* New York: Harper & Row, 1973.

Dyer, Evans, Lovell. *Putting Yourself Over in Business.* Englewood Cliffs, NJ: Prentice-Hall, Inc., 1957.

Fast, Julius. *Body Language.* New York: Pocket Books, Div. Simon & Schuster, 1975.

Flesch, Rudolph. *How to Write, Speak and Think More Effectively.* New York: New American Library, Signet, 1963.

Gardner, John W. *Excellence.* New York: Harper & Row, 1961.

Greene, Richard M. *How to Win With People.* Homewood, IL: Dow-Jones, Irwin, 1969.

Harriman, Bruce. "Up and Down the Communications Ladder." *Harvard Business Review,* Sept./Oct. 1974.

Harris, O. Jeff. *Managing People at Work: Concepts and Cases in Interpersonal Behavior.* New York: John Wiley & Sons, Inc., 1976.

Harris, Philip R., Dr. "Tools for Training: Group Dynamics Techniques." *Successful Meetings,* Dec. 1974.

_____ *Organization Dynamics,* 2nd ed. Los Angeles, CA: Tams Books, 1973.

Harris, Thomas A., M.D. *I'm OK—You're OK.* New York: Avon Books, Div. Hearst Corp., 1969.

Herzberg, Fred. *Work and the Nature of Man.* New York: World Publishing Co., 1966.

How to Manage a Real Estate Office Successfully. 1976 REALTORS® NATIONAL MARKETING INSTITUTE educational course.

James, Muriel. *The OK Boss.* Reading, MA: Addison-Wesley Publishing Co., 1976.

Jay, Antony. "How to Run a Meeting." *Harvard Business Review.* Mar./Apr. 1976.

_____ *Management and Machiavelli.* New York: Holt, Rinehart and Winston, 1967.

Leadership and Communications in Management. 1976 REALTORS® NATIONAL MARKETING INSTITUTE educational course.

Leavitt, Harold J. *Managerial Psychology,* rev. ed. Chicago: U. Chicago Press, 1965.

Maslow, Abraham H. *Motivation and Personality,* 2nd ed. New York: Harper & Row, 1970.

_____ *The Farther Reaches of the Mind.* New York: Viking Press, 1971.

Newman, Edwin. *Strictly Speaking.* Indianapolis, IN: Bobbs-Merrill Co., Inc., 1975.

_____ *A Civil Tongue.* _____, 1976.

Nichols and Stevens. *Are You Listening?* New York: McGraw-Hill Co., 1957.

Obtaining, Training and Retaining Sales Associates. 1976 REALTORS® NATIONAL MARKETING INSTITUTE educational course.

Odiorne, George S. *How Managers Make Things Happen.* Englewood Cliffs, NJ: Prentice-Hall, Inc., 1961.

Osborn, Alex F. *Applied Imagination,* 3rd rev. ed. New York: Scribner, 1963.

Parker, Paul P. *How To Use Tact and Skill in Handling People.* New York: Frederick Fell, Inc., 1959.

Pederson, Carlton A. and Wright, Milburn D. *Selling Principles and Methods,* 6th ed. Homewood, IL: Richard D. Irwin, Inc., 1976.

Personal Development: The Key to Professional Selling. 1976 REALTORS® NATIONAL MARKETING INSTITUTE educational course.

Prince, George M. *The Practice of Creativity.* New York: Macmillan Publishing Co., 1970.

Real Estate Ad-Views. Wellesley Hills, MA: Heritage Publishing Company.

"Real Estate Insider" newsletter. New York: Atcom, Inc.

REALTORS® NATIONAL MARKETING INSTITUTE. *Real Estate Office Management: People, Functions, Systems,* 1975.

_____ *Real Estate Advertising Ideas,* 1973.

_____ *real estate today®*, magazine published ten times a year.

_____ Training films, 1968-1976.

Riso, Ovid, Ed. *Sales Manager's Handbook,* 11th Ed. Chicago: Dartnell Corporation, 1970.

"Role Playing: The Better Way." *real estate today®*, Sept. 1975.

Salesmanship, a bi-monthly bulletin, Chicago, IL: Dartnell Corporation.

Schul, Bill D. *How To Be an Effective Leader.* Chicago, IL: Nelson Hall, 1975.

Seltz, David D. *Sales Contests and Incentive Programs.* Englewood Cliffs, NJ: Prentice-Hall, Inc., 1960.

Sigband, Norman B. *Management Communications for Decision Making.* Los Angeles: School-Industrial Press, Inc., 1973.

Townsend, Robert. *Up the Organization.* New York: Alfred A. Knopf, 1970.

Index

129